MW00941605

Copyright© 2017 Tracie Winn

ISBN-13: 978-1546311447

Acknowledgements

First and foremost, I thank God for giving me the courage to write this book. I would like to thank my family for their support throughout this entire process. I would also like to thank my friends, especially my sister circle, for all of the prayers and support. I would like to give special thanks to my sisters Rhenitha, Laketha, LaTissia, and Dominic. Thank you to my editor Yolanda Toney. This book is dedicated to everyone from my former church family and all that have suffered spiritual abuse.

Table of Contents

2006: Trading Chains for Chains 11

2007: Stay or Leave? 53

2008: Making Moves...72

2009: Change is Coming 97

2010: Time to Say Goodbye.. 145

Ten Signs of Spiritual Abuse 173

Foreword

In the course of your life, you will be tested. However, God will not allow the devil to destroy you. I was allowed to see this firsthand, when the devil attacked my oldest child. This was one of my lowest points and greatest tests. She was drawn into a cult at a stage in her life when she should have been growing. She was held back from growth by the group that she was involved with. This was a learning situation for both of us because we learned to trust God with all of our hearts and all of our being. When a test like this comes, you pray harder than you've ever prayed before. You pray not just for God's intervention, but to keep you from doing something that you will regret. During this period, I had to practice what I was teaching to others. I am so glad that she decided to tell her story. Hopefully, it will be a blessing and provide guidance to others who have gone through or are in a similar situation. So, read her story and embrace it. When God speaks to you, listen and obey.

Terris Winn Jr.

Introduction

"Some people can't last in a church and stay submitted to their pastor because they can't take the abuse!"

As the pastor shouted these words, the congregation clapped and called out its approval. The air filled with "amens" and "preach sirs". Immediately, I looked up at my pastor who sat in the pulpit of the church we were visiting. We exchanged glances with a smile and nod. Ironically, we had just spoken the night before about people who could not cut it in our church. This included those who had recently left and the individuals that kept getting into trouble. They were considered rebellious to our pastor's authority as a "chief apostle". Everything that the pastor of this church said lined up with what I had been taught for the past few years by my pastor. At this point, my mind was so warped that I thought abuse was okay. I thought being submitted to a pastor and ministry meant that I had to endure abuse.

I was involved with a Christian cult for four years. Compared to most known cults, my church was considered mainstream as far as beliefs go. We were taught about Jesus Christ and used only the Bible for reference. However, my pastor began to set himself up as an idol to us through fear, control, and manipulation.

After going through this experience, I realized that there is a huge misconception about what a cult is and who gets involved in one. When I was growing up, the word "cult" brought up images of Jonestown in Guyana and the Davidians in Waco, Texas. I thought only certain kinds of people joined cults. I thought a person had to be gullible or from a dysfunctional background to fall prey to the tactics of a cult. I thought something like that could never happen to me since I came from a Christian background and had two loving parents. My story is proof that this could be anybody's story.

I titled my book "Storefront" because of my personal experience with a church that met in storefronts, hotels, or homes instead of a traditional church building. This is the story of my experience with a particular church and does not reflect all churches that meet in non- traditional ways. This book is for anyone who has been affected by spiritual abuse. I want to dispel the lies of the devil and let someone know that abuse is never okay. God did not endorse it and He speaks extensively against it in the Bible. I pray that my testimony encourages and aids in healing. God bless you!

Storefront:
Hell in a Small Place

Tracie Winn

2006

Trading Chains for Chains

I feel that it is important to first explain where I was spiritually and emotionally prior to joining the church where I experienced spiritual abuse. This will help you understand why I was open to involvement with this particular church in the first place. No one gets up one day and says, "I think I will join a cult today." These groups prey on those who appear to be weak and vulnerable. When I was introduced to the church, I was in a very vulnerable state.

It all started in May 2006 when my walk with God radically changed. At the time, I was living in Birmingham while attending the University of Alabama in Birmingham. At this point in my life, I was sick and tired of living for God and the devil at the same time. I had been raised in church and had even rededicated my life to Christ when I arrived at college. However, for the next few years, I lived with one foot in the kingdom and one foot in the world. It was time to make a choice about whom I wanted to serve. Finally, I decided to live fully for God. I was not perfect, but I began to strive to live a holy life.

Before I could move forward, I had to do some housecleaning. Out went the people and things that were not conducive to my spiritual growth. Over a period of a few weeks, I was delivered from two major strongholds; fornication and alcohol. After God freed me, I felt that I was ready to walk in my assignment unhindered. I had always felt a call to ministry, but I could not shake the ways of the world off long enough to focus on what God wanted me to do.

So, I spent the rest of that summer getting closer to God and preparing for whatever He wanted me to do in ministry. Although I got closer to God, I became distanced from my friends in Birmingham. It got very lonely as I was asked to hang out less and less because I had changed my lifestyle. I longed for a group of Christian friends to hang out with and have clean fun.

In mid-July 2006, my best friend, Ashley, called me crying about the treatment that she was receiving at her church. She had been disrespected by not only the women there but the assistant pastor as well. She let me read an email that the assistant pastor, Pastor Williams, had sent her. I could not believe a pastor would send such ugly and hateful words to a member. In the email, he insulted her physical appearance numerous times. He claimed that he sent the email because he heard from an elder at the church that Ashley wanted to be with him. It was later found that this elder lied on Ashley. Instead of asking Ashley what the truth was, Pastor Williams assumed that the elder was telling the truth. Since I am very protective of friends and family, I decided to email him back. I firmly let him know that he was wrong and don't ever let me hear of him bothering my sister again. He did not respond.

Ashley had been attending the church since the beginning of 2006. She was introduced to the church by Elder Stevens. This was the elder who lied on her. They met while working for the same company. They and a couple of other people would drive from Huntsville to Atlanta to go to church every Sunday. I thought that they were crazy to go to church in another state when there were plenty of churches in Huntsville.

After Ashley joined, she talked to me about her church and her pastor often. A lot of red flags would pop up while she talked. I remember the earliest incident that she told me about concerning her pastor. Her pastor told the members that anyone who was late for church would have to pay a five dollar fine to get in. I remember thinking that God does not operate like that. The more that she told me about the church, the more upset I got with the people there.

Ashley would often invite me to visit, but I would always say no. However, after the incident with Pastor Williams, I decided to go check the church out. I went with the mindset that I was going to correct anybody who had hurt Ashley. As I mentioned before, I am fiercely protective of family and friends. This is a blessing, because I don't mind being there for people. This is also a curse, because I continue to be there even in situations when I should walk away. My loyalty is what kept me tied to the church for four years when I should have left.

I decided to visit the following Sunday. A couple of days before I went, Ashley called and said that her pastor had a prophetic word for me. She also told me that he wanted to discuss hosting a women's conference with me. She had told him about the women's ministry we had together. At this point, I had not done anything ministry related. We were still in the developing stages. I had not even preached my first sermon yet. I was blown away at this door that I felt God was opening for me. I told her that it was fine if we met with him, but I still had not forgotten my original reason for visiting. Looking back, that was a horrible reason to visit a church.

But, I felt that I had to defend Ashley. I even brought my friend, Candice, along in case I needed back up.

When we pulled up to the address that I was given, my mouth hung in shock. We were in front of a hotel in College Park.

"Is this where the church is? Inside of a hotel?" Candice asked in disbelief.

"This is the address that Ashley gave me," I said. I was stunned as well.

At this point, we were not sure if we wanted to get out and go in. We had sat for almost an hour in downtown Atlanta traffic and were already running late. We were also skeptical after finding out the church was in a hotel. After sitting in the car about fifteen minutes, we decided to go inside. We got out and headed towards the entrance of the hotel. Even though we were in the parking lot, we could hear drums pounding and someone shouting on a microphone. We followed the sounds of the music and came to a stop in front of a conference room door. The door had a handmade sign taped to it that bore the church's name, Anointed Revival Center. When I pushed the door open, someone dressed in all black rushed by me yelling into a microphone. We stepped into the room and took a moment to look around.

In one corner, I saw Ashley dancing in the spirit to the music being played by the band. Then, I noticed that there were people laid all around on the floor speaking in tongues. Then, the man in black (whom I found out later was Bishop Davis, the pastor) began to prophesy to people and lay hands on them. I watched as those that he touched dropped like flies to the ground. I had never seen anything like that before except on television. Candice and I just stood there taking it all in.

Finally, we made our way to a row of seats. We did not sit though. We could not sit because we were so mesmerized by what was going on around us.

Suddenly, Bishop Davis turned to me and said, "Tracie, come here. The Lord has a word for you."

Meanwhile, I stepped forward nervously wondering how he knew who I was. Ironically, he began to tell me things that confirmed what God had told me. He also addressed situations that nobody knew about except God. At that moment, I did not feel so alone. Honestly, I felt comforted and understood. As I stood there with tears streaming down my face like a waterfall, Bishop laid his hands on me. I immediately felt a rush of heat from head to toe that seemed like the fire Jeremiah, the prophet, described in his bones. The next thing I knew, Elder Stevens was holding on to me as

I leaped and praised God. She hurriedly wrapped my waist with a white sheet. I found out later that I had shouted so hard until my skirt slipped down. I had literally praised out of my clothes! At this point, Bishop walked over and laid hands on me again. This time I fell to the floor and began speaking in tongues. I just laid there and let God have His way. Inasmuch, I could feel healing and deliverance taking place in me.

After about ten minutes, I got up from the floor to go back to my seat. When, I got there Candice was in tears as she told me that she had received prayer and a prophetic word just like I did. Then, Bishop Davis called service to order. Unknowingly, I thought we were running late, but church had not even started yet! I was quite impressed that the church was extremely fiery before service had even started. To my surprise, they had only had prayer at that point.

Time progressed, and we went through the rest of the service. If I may be honest, I enjoyed everything about it. The praise and worship was amazing. I couldn't believe how gifted and anointed Bishop Davis was! To this day, I haven't heard anyone sing or operate in the Spirit like him. I loved how he totally relied on the Holy Spirit to lead us through the service instead of rigidly following a program. Among everything that took place, I enjoyed the sermon most of all. I felt like it was a word from God that was designed for me specifically. Hence, Bishop preached from Isaiah 43:18-19. Because I was in a place in my life where I was tired of the old and ready for something new to begin in my life, I desired new friends and a godly relationship among other things. I was so tired of being around the wrong people who were pulling me down instead of building me up. In addition to longing for a renewed sense of identity, I was ready to go to the next level spiritually. Therefore, I knew it was time to step out on the things that God had given me to do. Relentlessly, I sat there as the pastor preached and wondered if this church was the place that I needed to plant new spiritual seed, so I could achieve the things that I desired.

As soon as church was dismissed, Ashley and I walked out in the hallway to talk. While we stood there talking by the snack machine, Bishop Davis walked up to us. Ashley then formally introduced us. He was so friendly and well-dressed. I remember thinking how handsome he was. After Ashley introduced us, he insisted that Candice and I join him and the other members for dinner. Since we were not in a hurry to get back to Birmingham, I told him that we would join him and the others.

Before we could leave the hotel, Ashley said that she had to go help the other members clean up the conference room where the church service was held. I watched from the door as members took down banners and put up chairs. I had never seen anybody set up and take down a church. Because of this and other unfortunate things that would soon unfold, I later referred to the church as "The Circus Church".

When we got in our cars to leave, I pulled out to get behind Bishop's car so I could follow him. Ashley then informed me that the cars had to travel in a certain order. For instance, Bishop's car had to go first followed by Elder Stevens. No one was ever allowed to drive in front of Bishop. However, Ashley said I could fall in line behind Elder Stevens since I was a minister. All I could do was laugh when she told me this. I could not believe that there were rules, even about the way the church members drove up the road.

Meanwhile, we arrived at the restaurant, which was not far from the hotel, and were seated. I sat directly across from Bishop as he requested. During the gathering, I chatted with him and the other members as we enjoyed our food. Surprisingly, I really enjoyed talking to him. It was refreshing to see him as a regular person and not in preacher mode. We laughed and talked for hours. I felt like we had made a connection spiritually and naturally.

The fellowship with the church that night was exactly what I needed. Despite observing a few things that were weird to me, I saw that they were like a real family. This church family seemed to be really close. I rarely saw fellow church members at my former church congregate and/or commune outside of church with one another on purpose.

As the night went on, I put the disturbing rumors that I had heard about the church out of my mind. I even had a decent conversation with Pastor Williams. We never once mentioned the email.

As we walked to our cars after dinner, Bishop pulled me away from the group to talk to me alone.

"So...when are you coming back?" he asked.

"I don't know...soon" I replied.

"Okay. Well I will see you Sunday then", he said smiling.

"We'll see" I said as I smiled back.

We talked a few minutes longer, and then Candice and I got in the car to leave.

For some apparent reason, I smiled all of the way home that night. I could not stop thinking about Bishop or the church. I later told Ashley how I really enjoyed her church and meeting her pastor. I told her that I felt a connection with him, but not to say anything. I wanted the ball to be in his court since he was the man. If he liked me, he would have to make the first move.

After my initial visit, I kept going back Sunday after Sunday for about a month. Although I was not officially a member, I was getting closer to joining with each visit. Honestly, a lot of it had to do with what was happening between me and Bishop Davis.

A couple of weeks after I visited the first time, Ashley called me with a question.

"Bishop wants to know if you like him because, he likes you," she said.

I stumbled away from my closet where I had been hanging clothes so I could sit down on my bed. I could barely process it all. Of course, he had given hints that he was interested, but officially hearing that he liked me was something else. After Ashley reported the conversation that had occurred between her and Bishop, she told me that he wanted me to call him. I told her to tell him to call me if he really liked me and wanted to talk.

Almost half an hour later, my phone rang. My caller ID showed that it was an Atlanta number. I knew it was him. I took a deep breath before answering the phone.

"Hello?"

"So I guess you know that I like you now," he began. "I just want you to know that I'm not looking for a fling. I'm looking for a wife. I feel like we have a connection."

Then, he started to talk to me about joining the church. He said he was looking for classy, intelligent, and stable people to bring into the church.

"It takes a special lady to be a first lady," he added.

This was the first, but not last time that he would use the "you're my wife" card to try to manipulate me. After he said his spill, he asked if I liked him as well. I told him yes and he began to shout hallelujah at the top of his lungs. He told me he felt like running up the road because he was so happy. We decided to get to know each other and see how the Lord led us. His next question was asking me to be over the women's ministry. He said that he was not pleased with the current women's leader, whom was Elder Stevens. He also said that the position was best suited for a first lady anyway. He kept saying how powerful he believed that I was in the spirit and how I would make a good first lady to walk beside him in ministry. Although I did not recognize it then, he was manipulating me with flattery. He knew that I desired most to be used by the Lord and be a wife.

I learned over the years that when Bishop wanted something, he did not stop until he got it. It did not matter what he had to do or say to get it. With each of the members, he would become whatever they wanted him to be just for him to get what he wanted from them. We had all experienced hurt and rejection. Likewise, we all desired love and acceptance. To some, he was a father-figure. To others, he was a friend. To women like me, he was a potential husband. Over the next three years, he gave me just enough of himself to keep me around. He dangled that carrot of marriage in my face until I finally gave up on us ever being together.

Over the next few weeks, we continued to talk on the phone regularly. We also began to spend time together outside of the church. However, we were never alone. We were always accompanied by Pastor Williams and Ashley. Sometimes other members would come with us too. I remember one time when we all went to the movies together. Instead of sitting by me, he sat across the room with Pastor Williams. But, he texted me the entire time which I thought was weird. Although it frustrated me that we were never alone, I accepted it because I thought he just wanted to remain accountable by going on group outings.

I was enjoying getting to know him better as well as everyone else. I felt more and more at home in Atlanta each time I went. For most weekends, I spent the night at the home of Candice's mother. Sometimes Bishop would invite me and Ashley to stay the weekend with him and Pastor Williams at their apartment. We would stay up and watch movies and play games. They also loved to prank call us in the middle of the night. Bishop and Pastor Williams were so funny and so much fun. Those visits made me want to move to Atlanta. It was extremely hard to leave everybody at the end of those weekends. I loved how close we all were. We all went everywhere together-church, the movies, the mall, and out to eat, etc. It was exactly what I needed.

Each time I talked to Bishop, he would pressure me into becoming a member and moving to Atlanta. Late one night in mid-August, Bishop texted me and said that he needed me to become part of the ministry immediately and take over the women's ministry. He said that it was an urgent situation and he needed my help. I felt so honored that he needed me. I did not want to let him down, so I knew what I had to do.

As a result, I joined the church officially that Sunday. It was a bittersweet moment because Elder Stevens was not there and had not been told that I was replacing her. I wholeheartedly felt bad for her, but I was glad to have the position. I remember Bishop and Pastor Williams laughing and saying how her jaw would drop when she heard that I had taken her spot. They kept on joking about how upset she was going to be. Unfortunately, in my immaturity I laughed along with them.

Soon after I joined, I began to see the other side of Bishop for myself. I had been told about it, but had not experienced it. One of the first incidents took place a couple of Sundays after I joined.

I found out on a Saturday morning that my aunt and uncle were coming up to Birmingham from Florida the next day. Since I rarely got to see them, I decided not to go to Atlanta that weekend.

I got a call from Bishop that evening wanting to know if I had made it to Atlanta yet. I would usually drive down on Saturday and stay through Sunday or Monday, so he was expecting me that night. I let him know that I had family coming to visit and would not be coming to Atlanta.

After he heard my reasoning, he asked me, "How do you plan on being a first lady if you are not at church on Sundays?"

"It's just one Sunday. I never get to see my aunt and uncle. They live in Florida. I promise I'll be there from now on. I just really want to see my family. My parents, brother, and sister are even coming down from Huntsville," I explained.

"I need you here with me...to have my back," he asserted.

He always asked me to pray for him during services. He claimed that it helped him to minister at his best. Just like a candle waiting to be lit, his plea was all that I needed to hear. If he needed me, I had to be there. My family would just have to wait. After all, I wanted to show him that I could be a good wife. I wanted to be the kind of wife that put her husband first before anyone or anything.

Unbeknownst to me, this was his first step in isolating me from my family. Deceitfully, he also took attention from God. His argument was that I needed to be at church for him. Not one time did he mention being there for the Lord. Obviously, he wanted to gain all of my loyalty.

After I hung up the phone, I felt nothing but guilt. I felt bad for ditching my family, but even worse that I had put Bishop in a position where he felt like he could not rely on me. I told myself that night that I would do my best to never let him down again.

Soon after, more concerns began to come up about Bishop and the ministry. I found out that Bishop had an awfully bad temper. For instance, I had witnessed him yell on more than one occasion at his armor bearers. He yelled at them if he didn't have chapstick or if his water was not the right brand. The armor bearers were responsible for carrying a bag of specific items everywhere that we went so that

Bishop always had what he needed. In addition to the obvious, the armor bearers were also responsible for providing the drinks and any other items that Bishop requested out of their own pockets for every service or outing. We had to run to the store sometimes before or during a service to buy Chap Stick, gum, or more towels for Bishop. And...the armor bearers had to wash the towels after each service and take Bishop's robes to be dry cleaned. Once early on, I took one of the armor bearers to pick up Bishop's robe from the dry cleaner's. When we got there, they had closed early for the weekend. The armor bearer's eyes filled with tears as she told me that she was going to be in big trouble with Bishop for not getting the robe.

"He's going to kill me", she cried.

"You didn't know they closed early on Fridays. Why can't he just wear a different robe", I subtly asked.

"You just don't understand", she ~~said~~ professed while shaking her head.

She was right. At that time, I didn't see what the big deal was. But...I soon learned.

Before coming to the church, I had never seen or heard of armor bearers. They were basically Bishop's servants. There were four of them, including Pastor Williams, when I first joined the church. They were required to follow Bishop

...er he went. They even accompanied him to run daily errands or ran the errands for him. Additionally, they drove him around, carried his bags, cleaned his apartment, had his suits and robes dry cleaned, carried his Bible, and brought him Gatorade in wine glasses while he preached. Ridiculously, they even fanned him after he finished ministering. They also could not leave and go home until Bishop released them from being on duty. This went for the ministers as well. Once, I left before being released and received a series of long, ugly text messages as a result. Being on call for Bishop took up so much time that keeping a job, going to school, or having interests outside of the church became difficult for the armor bearers. Bishop had it included in the church by-laws that they were required to accompany him to every engagement: no exceptions. I saw an armor bearer lose his or her job more than once because Bishop made them choose him or her choose between going to work or going somewhere with him.

I also began to notice that the most minor offenses would set him off. He wanted everything to be a certain way. This meant that everything needed to be his way no matter what we thought or felt. Noncompliance would result in him losing his temper. For example, he would throw wine glasses across the room or beat his desk with his fist. One night during a church meeting he got mad and hit the podium so hard he broke it. After losing his temper, he would then go on as if nothing happened. It was startling how he could go from raving mad one second to being nice and gentle in the next. It was truly a Jekyll and Hyde situation. I was concerned, but grateful that he had not directed that anger towards me...yet.

In September, we had our first women's event called 50 Women in White. Bishop asked me to coordinate it and emailed me a lengthy list of instructions concerning the event. In the email, he stated that he was turning the service over to me because he believed I was capable. Then, next came the list telling me exactly what to do. I was instructed to ask each female member for twenty-five dollars. Each female guest was asked to give ten dollars. Another requirement was that fifty or more women be present. He also asked that all the women of the ministry mime or dance together. On top of everything else he had already done, he even chose and booked the speaker for the event. I soon began to see that he did not relinquish control to other people whom he had appointed.

We later bumped heads over the ladies' outing that he asked me to plan. He wanted all the ladies to get together and do something on Saturday afternoon without the men.

Our disagreement happened when we were on the phone one night. I was telling him that the women had decided to go out to eat and fellowship. He wanted to know exactly where we were going so he could come. I thought he was just joking and being playful by wanting to come where I was. I joked back that he couldn't come. I reminded him that it was for ladies only.

"I'm the pastor. You can't tell me where I can and can't go. I don't care if you are the first lady," he said while laughing.

After we laughed, we moved on to another topic. I thought that would be the end of it. I soon learned that most of the time Bishop wouldn't say anything right away if something bothered him. He would keep thinking about it and analyzing it. Then, sometimes weeks or months later, he would explode on you.

A week before the women's service, I received a call from him.

"I will not be controlled by you! My momma wants to know who you think you are telling me where I can and can't go. How are you gonna tell me I can't come out to eat with y'all and I'm the pastor", he yelled as soon as I answered the phone.

I quickly apologized for offending him. Inasmuch, I explained that I thought he was joking about coming to the women's dinner since he stated in the email he sent that the outing was for women only. While he characterized me as being controlling, I was accused of not doing my share of the coordination because I asked one of the sisters to help me find a nice restaurant for the outing. Since she was an Atlanta native, I felt she would know better than me where we could go. Therefore, I apologized again, and I told him he was welcome to come eat with us.

The day of the outing, Bishop and Pastor Williams met us at the hotel where the speaker for the event would be staying. We were meeting to make sure her room was up to par and leave her a fruit basket. I noticed that Bishop stayed in the car while Pastor Williams came upstairs to talk to us. After he looked over the room, Pastor Williams pulled me to the side to talk.

"Bishop didn't come up here because he is offended with you," he conveyed.

"I thought everything was okay since we talked the other night. I apologized to him when we were on the phone," I humbly explained.

"You should probably go downstairs and try to apologize again," he suggested.

So, I went downstairs to their car and knocked on the window. Bishop rolled the window down.

"Yes?"

I could tell he was upset by the disgusted look on his face. I was so nervous, but I managed to get my words out.

"Bishop, I'm so sorry for offending you. It wasn't my intention", I said.

I would come to repeat these words to Bishop on a regular basis at every perceived slight over the next few years. After I apologized, he smiled and let me know that he accepted my apology. He, along with the men of the church, did end up coming to the restaurant. Although they sat in a separate room, Bishop still kept coming to our section wanting to see what we were doing and to flirt with me.

This behavior became a pattern with us. He would find something to be offended with me about. Then, I would beg his forgiveness. The fact that he was not always this way is what kept me around. The good times outweighed the bad. He called everyday to check on me. If we weren't talking on the phone, we were texting each other. Sometimes, he would text just to say he missed me and that he wished that I was in Atlanta with him. He often talked about coming to Birmingham to spend the night with me. Then, he would tell me he wanted to sleep in my bed instead of on the couch. I would shut that down because I was not trying to fall in sin with him. Why I still wanted to be with him, I don't know. I guess it felt good to be needed and chosen by him. I also loved that he was very protective. During the planning of the women's event, the manager of one of the featured groups threatened me because I wouldn't give him the amount of money he demanded and sign a contract. He had previously told me the group would perform for free and then changed his mind. Bishop lost it when I told him how the guy had disrespected me. He called the manager up and went off on him. He and Pastor Williams threatened to beat the guy up. Like a lock on a safe, he made me feel secure and protected.

Meanwhile, the women's program ended up being just okay. It made me feel like all the drama we went through was in vain. We even had a "hostage" situation. A local pastor who served as our overseer was asked to take up the offering. She told the ministers from her church to go guard the doors. Then, she told us that a certain amount of money needed to be raised and nobody was going anywhere until they got it. Almost thirty minutes later, someone wrote a check, and we were all released to go home. The only good thing that happened was that I made a connection to Pastor's cousin that preached for the service. She was among the few who was authentically tapped into the spirit that night.

A couple of weeks later, I was given my next assignment as the women's leader. I was delegated to get the women to go in together on a gift for the pastoral anniversary of the overseer of our church. Bishop instructed me to get her a gift certificate for a certain amount from her favorite restaurant. Since we needed the gift for the upcoming Sunday, I immediately contacted the women of the church. I asked each woman if she could contribute towards the gift certificate. They all confirmed that they could. I let them know that I would collect the money when I got there on Saturday. When I arrived in Atlanta on Saturday night, only one person besides me had money to give towards the gift. I was devastated because I didn't have the money personally to make up for what was missing.

That night, I sat in the living room of one of the ministers, Min. Marlene. I kept going over in my mind how to tell Bishop that I was not able to get the gift certificate. As I was sitting there, Min. Marlene came down the steps and asked if I was okay. I guess she noticed the worried look on my face. I explained to her what happened with the gift. She apologized for not being able to help since she was not working at the time. I told her it was okay and that I was just worried about letting Bishop down. Then, she said something that stunned me.

"I am so tired of Bishop messing with y'all little girl's minds. He ought to be ashamed," she professed.

"What do you mean by that?" I innocently asked.

She went on to tell me that she was tired of watching Bishop manipulate and control the women of the church. She was especially mad about one of the young ladies, Sabrina, because this particular young lady was a relative of hers.

"I see how he is with them, and now he is doing the same thing with you. He only does this with the ones that he feels that he can control. He makes them think he likes them just so he can use them. He knows better than to come at me like that. He calls Sabrina every morning asking her to go run errands for him. She doesn't have a car, so she spends most of the day on the bus running around for him and spending her own money on what he wants. When he says jump, she asks how high. I feel so sorry for y'all little girls. He is just playing with y'all and running game. I didn't want to say anything, but I had to. You seem like such a nice girl."

I sat there shocked as I listened to her. She told me that she didn't agree with most of the teachings and rules. She also admitted that she sometimes thought of going to another church but stayed because she wholeheartedly appreciated Bishop allowing her to operate as a minister. For almost an hour, she confided in me how she felt about the ministry. Finally, she got up to go to her bedroom. I sat there in the dark trying to process everything that I had just been told. I finally convinced myself that what she said was not true.

It is different with me, I thought as I grabbed my phone to call Bishop.

When he answered the phone, I explained to him what happened with the gift. I apologized for not contacting him sooner. For a moment, there was silence on his end.

"I asked you to do a task... and it's not done," he said. I could tell by his tone he was getting upset.

"Well, it's too late for you to do anything about it now. I'll have Pastor Williams take care of it in the morning", he pronounced.

I apologized to him and tried to explain how none of the ladies, except one, had money to give towards the gift. All he said was that he would talk to me at church the next day. Once he finished his reprimanding me, he hung up the phone.

I was crushed thinking about how I had let him down once again. On top of that, I didn't even get a chance to ask him about what Min. Marlene had told me concerning him and the other females in the ministry.

Shortly after that, I did get to address what was told to me by Min. Marlene. He laughed and told me that she was lying on him because he didn't want her. He told me at one time or another every woman in the ministry had come on to him except Ashley. I hung up that night feeling relieved that what I was told was not true. Therefore, I thought that was the end of it. But...I was wrong.

A couple of days later, I received a text message from Bishop telling me that I was messy and untrustworthy. I called him immediately to ask him what the text was about. He sent me to voice mail. Over time, I learned that this was his normal behavior. He would drop a bomb on you and then not talk to you. After he sent me to voice mail the second time, I decided to text him back. As I was texting him, he was calling me.

"Hello," I answered nervously.

"Hey," he uttered with no emotion.

"What's going on? I got your text," I said.

"I am really upset about the conversation that you had with Min. Marlene the other night. How could you sit up all night and listen to somebody dog me? I know you probably talked about me too. What you did was messy, and y'all are sowing discord in the ministry. I talked to my mom about it and she agrees that you are messy and probably shouldn't be a member of the church. One thing I can't stand is a messy woman. And if you call yourself wanting to be with me, you can't be going around sowing discord. Now tell me again exactly what happened!" Bishop exclaimed.

By this point, my head was spinning. Just a couple of nights before, we had laughed about the situation. Now here I was being accused of being messy and talking about him to others. I was also embarrassed that he had told his mother that I was messy.

I responded, "I told you the other night that Min. Marlene just brought up some things about you and the ministry to me. I did listen to what she had to say but, I didn't say anything against you. And I'm sorry that I didn't say anything to defend you. Honestly, I was just so shocked by what she was saying that I didn't know what to say".

I paused and waited for his response hoping that he knew that I was telling the truth.

"Well Min. Marlene, is that how it went down?" he asked.

"Bishop we both said some things we probably shouldn't have and I'm sorry." a voice on the line confessed.

It was Min. Marlene. Bishop had us on three way. I didn't know if I felt more betrayed by him having her on the line or her lying on me. At that point, I was fed up. I was not going to sit there and be accused of doing something that I did not do. Without any doubt, I started defending myself, and Bishop didn't like it. The next thing I knew, we were yelling at each other while Min. Marlene just sat there and listened. Finally, Bishop said he would talk to me later when I was not being disrespectful. Then, he hung up on me.

The next morning, he called and apologized for yelling and for having Min. Marlene on the phone. I apologized as well for yelling at him. I let him know that I felt hurt by the accusations. He told me that he knew I wasn't being messy. He claimed that he was just testing her to see if she would tell the truth or lie on me. I didn't stop to consider that if he really thought it was all her, then he wouldn't have told his mother that I was messy. I was just glad that we had made up and could move on.

For the next few months, we all went through ups and downs with each other. There was so much tension between me and the other ladies. It was such a struggle to plan anything concerning the women because most of them did not care for me. Honestly, I did not trust any of them except Ashley. Likewise, I began to resent some of them as well because we viewed each other as competition for a non-existent position as Bishop's wife. I wish that we all had realized that none of us ever had a chance of being with him.

It was around this time that Bishop began breaking down the friendship between me and Ashley. It all started one Sunday when Bishop cancelled evening service. Ashley and I decided to take advantage of that and get on the road while it was still early. After driving awhile, we decided to stop and get something to eat. While standing in line at the restaurant, Bishop began to send us several text messages back to back. He was upset that we had left Atlanta early and didn't go out to eat with him. He told us that we should be eating with our shepherd (him) and not by ourselves. He didn't like members being alone together. I feel like he was afraid of us getting together and comparing notes about negative aspects of the ministry. This is exactly what Ashley and I did once we sat down with our food. We discussed the things about the ministry that concerned us. We were tired of the constant drama and being rebuked for every little thing. However, we decided to stay put. Bishop was like the father Ashley never had. As for me, he was husband material. Bishop would constantly tell me that my destiny was tied to him and the ministry in order to keep me there. He told me if I ever left, I would be out of God's will.

After that incident, Bishop began to work on sowing discord between me and Ashley. It would be years before she and I discussed the negativity again. We learned how to suppress our emotions and keep things bottled up, eventually became like robots. We learned to speak and do only what we were told by Bishop.

As the months went on I became assimilated into the ministry. Bishop liked me in skirt suits and high heels. So, I began to wear that for him. Almost every week I was buying new suits and shoes to look a certain way for him. Eventually, he had us all dressed the same. He claimed this would establish us as a unified body of Christ. Bishop told us what to wear for most church services and for fellowship with other churches. We all wore the same colors wherever we went. The ministers were also required to wear clergy shirts every first Sunday. Not wearing the assigned outfit would cause us to be harshly rebuked. Sometimes Bishop rebuked people during the church service over the microphone. Other times he would just yell at us in his office. The female ministers and armor bearers were expected to wear stockings and heels even on a casual outing. We also were required to wear skirts and dresses only in and out of church in order to operate as ministers. Later, he wanted the other female members to dress this way as well. Our casual wear was usually head to toe black because that is how Bishop dressed most of the time. Or, we wore black tops and long denim skirts. At first, the women were told to wear no makeup or jewelry. This was hard for me because I loved both. I felt naked leaving the house with a bare face and no jewelry. Thankfully, he diverted and let us wear stud earrings and nothing more as far as jewelry. The no makeup rule changed one Sunday when he got up to make a special announcement.

"I know I told you ladies that makeup is not allowed. But, I have decided to change that rule because some of you need to have on some makeup. So, I will allow y'all to wear a little bit of makeup. Don't get carried away though," he reprimanded.

I wasn't even shocked when he got up and basically implied that some of the women looked ugly without makeup. He got up and said whatever he felt like saying. He didn't care if it hurt or offended someone.

On top of dress requirements, we also had financial obligations on top of regular tithes and offerings. I found out that we had two required fees for the ministry each month. Every first Sunday, we gave 30 dollars to the church building fund. This money could not be saved up since it went to hotel fees and paying musicians. Every third Sunday was Founder's Day. It was a special church service to celebrate Bishop. We would bring him gifts, and a couple of people would be selected to get up and speak about him as a tribute.

For instance, we would invite a guest speaker and others to sing, dance, etc. We also were required to each give Bishop 40 dollars. If we did not pay these dues, Pastor Williams would hunt us down after church and ask us how soon we would have the money to give to Bishop. Outside of that money, we were often encouraged to give more and more to the church. Bishop would say, "Don't give your rent money." Then, he would turn around and beg people to give sacrificial offerings. He would use manipulation and guilt to get money from people. One Sunday, he had me drive a visitor to an ATM during service so she could get money to give to him after he manipulated her. He also once tried to guilt me into giving him my tax refund money during church service.

"Some of y'all just got your refund and won't even give it to God," he implied while looking directly at me.

I had already given in the offering, but he wanted it all.

He would tell us to give what we had put aside for other things and God would multiply it back to us. No matter how much we gave, it seemed there was never enough money for the ministry to operate. Sometimes, I would have to use my credit card to pay for our hotel meeting room. Bishop and Pastor Williams would promise to pay me back but never would. Over the years we moved around from hotel to hotel and building to building due to eviction and complaints about our church. We even had to have church sometimes at Bishop's apartment. Sadly, we became spiritual gypsies.

I also found out some unspoken rules. These were the things I learned as I went along. This usually happened after I broke a rule that I didn't know existed. Not only did we have to drive in a certain order, but we had to eat in a certain order. When we dined at a restaurant, Bishop always ordered first. If it was a buffet, he fixed his plate first. When we had church potlucks, there was a separate table for Bishop, Pastor Williams, and visiting pastors. The ministers and armor bearers had to serve as waiters to the head table as if it was a restaurant. We served the food and refilled drinks. We also had to stand on post by the table in case they needed us to get something. Once we were released by Bishop, we could go eat. We also had to walk behind him, even in the mall, at all times. The main rules were not to question Bishop or discuss the negative aspects of the ministry with each other or outsiders. We were taught to follow and obey Bishop whether we agreed or not. We were constantly being taught about scriptures concerning submission to authority. I was scared to even discuss the ministry with God in prayer because I was scared that Bishop would find out since he was a prophet. We were often told that if anyone from outside the church said something negative about the church, it was persecution. This even went for our families. Anyone that didn't agree with something or questioned Bishop was viewed as a rebellious troublemaker. Bishop would humiliate those that were considered troublemakers from the pulpit. People that asked questions didn't last long in the ministry.

I also learned that we were required to obtain Bishop's permission before we did anything for church or in our personal lives. We consulted him about where we lived, worked, and what we wore. We also had to ask him before missing church for any reason. I had to ask permission just to go on vacation with my family. He would also give me grief about going to church with my parents for Mother's Day and Father's Day. He definitely didn't allow us to visit other churches unless he was there too or we had been asked to preach there. Even then, we had to get his permission to go preach at another church although we had a green light from God. I remember once God used me at a revival service that I was attending with a friend who was ministering. I was nervous because, I had not asked Bishop in advance if I could just go and support her. During the service, I was asked by a pastor to come up in the pulpit and share whatever God was laying on my heart to say. I went up and ministered what God told me to say. However, a musician that was Bishop's friend was in the audience. He promptly texted Bishop to inform him that I had just ministered. When I left the service, I had several texts from Bishop rebuking me for not asking him first. He said that I was not allowed to minister to anyone without his permission. He expected me to step out in the middle of that service to call and ask if it was okay to speak. He was so controlling when it came to our gifts and callings. He once made me and Ashley leave a person's home where we were praying for them simply because we hadn't asked his permission to go out witnessing that day.

Although there were things going on that I didn't agree with, I can say that there were good things going on with the ministry. I was so grateful for the teaching and training that I was receiving from Bishop. He was training me on how to operate in ministry. Before I met Bishop, I didn't know basic ministry etiquette. We learned about the different offices of the church and how to operate in our spiritual gifts. Also, the church reminded me of the early church in Acts. We were like one big family. We ate, prayed, studied, and fasted together regularly. Miracles, signs, and wonders were also commonplace. I saw things that I had never seen done before in my previous churches. I saw people come into church on walkers and leave leaping and running. I saw deaf ears opened. I saw people healed of various diseases.

Around December of 2006, certain things came to a head. After only being there four months, I decided it was time to leave the church. It all started in November when we found out that Bishop was having an installation service in December. The ministers were told that once we completed minister's training, which had been going on a couple of months, we would receive our ministerial licenses. I also found out that I would be preaching my first sermon a couple of weeks from then. What should have been an exciting time quickly became anything but that.

Meanwhile, I was asked to coordinate the reception for the installation. I thought that it would be simple to get ten women to come together to serve punch and cake. I was so wrong. Planning this event was complicated because almost every woman involved was competing to be the first lady of the church. Some, including me, had been told that they were. I did not know at the time that Bishop was telling some of the women the same things he told me. That is why there was so much resistance when I stepped into the position of leading the women.

As we moved forward in planning the event, most of the women would not cooperate with me. Once again, I found it especially difficult to get the women to contribute financially. Bishop had instructed me to get the women to give a certain amount towards the reception. I later found out that the women thought that I and not Bishop was the one asking for money. The only ones that really offered help were a group of women that did not belong to our church but regularly fellowshipped with us. I was instructed by Pastor Williams not to accept their help because, they were not members yet. He thought that I was asking for their money and did not believe me when I said that they had called me and offered it.

At this point nothing was coming together because, there was only so much that I could do from Huntsville and with limited funds. Finally, a couple of days before the installation I got a call from Pastor Williams.

"Praise the Lord Minister Tracie. This is Pastor Williams. I am calling on behalf of Bishop Davis. He wanted me to let you know that he is not pleased with you or how you are planning the event."

While Pastor Williams was speaking, I could hear Bishop yelling in the background. Bishop was afraid sometimes to confront people. He would get intimidated and get Pastor Williams or one of the other ministers to do it for him. I had to fight his battles several times because he was not man enough to do so.

I was stunned. I went right into my apologizing routine so they would not be mad, and I could get out of being in trouble with him. I began trying to explain the difficulties that I had been having with getting full cooperation from the women.

"Don't worry about it," he assured.

He then let me know that Sabrina and another minister named Brittany would take care of everything. He then hung up on me. I sat there stunned and looking at my phone. I could not believe that I had just been dismissed and hung up on like I was nothing. It also bothered me that Bishop did not talk to me directly but, chose to yell in the background while Pastor Williams talked to me. I decided to try and call Bishop and talk to him about the situation one on one. I tried to call him several times, but he would not answer the phone. Since I was feeling hurt and rejected, I called one of my close friends, Tameka, and let her know what had happened.

"Tracie, you have to take heed to these red flags that keep popping up with this guy," Tameka told me. "You shouldn't pursue a relationship with a man that won't talk to you directly or answer the phone when there is a problem. I honestly believe he is playing you. He is playing with your heart and your mind."

I thought about what Tameka told me, so I decided to leave Bishop and the church alone. I knew that I didn't deserve to be mistreated by him or anybody else. I was tired of having to apologize for every minor thing that offended him. After making my decision, I texted Bishop and let him know that I was unhappy and would be leaving the ministry. He called me immediately wanting to know why I was upset. I calmly explained how I felt about everything. I let him know that Tameka had given me some advice on the situation. That was a huge mistake. He got angry when I mentioned her name. I found out as time went on that Pastor did not want us seeking counsel outside of him. He felt threatened by those that could see him and the ministry for what they were: a fraud and a mess. Then, he started begging me not to leave. When I still insisted that I was done with him, he put his mom on the phone. That was not the last time that he used that tactic to get me to stay. She told me that they didn't want me to go and how much everybody in the ministry loved me. Then, he got back on the phone.

"See even your mother in law doesn't want you to go," he reaffirmed.

By the time I hung up with them, I had changed my mind about leaving. Then, he sent me a text saying that he loved me and didn't want me to leave. That really sealed it for me. He loved me! He had never said that to me before. Looking back, I can't believe that I fell for that. But, that is what happens when you are desperate for love. You take it any way that you can get it until you love yourself enough to walk away. The following evening after work, I was on the highway headed to Atlanta for the weekend. When I arrived, everyone was kind of distant with me. They weren't cold, but not friendly either. The next day, everyone was nice to me again when they needed me to drive all over Atlanta to run errands.

The night of the Installation Service was very memorable. First, I received my ministerial license which was awesome. However, the service lasted several hours. It was hijacked by a visiting pastor that felt the need to testify for hours and prophesy doom to almost every person present. She was telling people they were going to get in car accidents and develop various diseases. Then, she started testifying that a lot of popular songs and movies were her ideas first but, the FBI bugged her phone and stole the information. I couldn't believe this lady. Everyone felt drained in every way listening to her ramble. Once the service ended, all of the guests rushed to leave. Since everyone had left, no one came to the reception. Only three people (outside of the members of the church) saw the decorations the women argued about before the service. Only three people saw the cake with Bishop's picture on it that we yelled at the staff of Publix about because, the picture was initially too small for Bishop. I can't blame everyone for leaving though. The service started at 5 p.m. and ended at 10 p.m.

Just when I thought all the drama had blown over, I woke up the next morning to another helping of it. I found out from Pastor Williams that one of the women was upset that I had asked for financial contribution for the event. Of course, Pastor Williams did not tell her that I was just following orders from him and Bishop. By this point, I wished that I had not even come back. After rebuking me, Pastor Williams asked what gift the women had for Bishop. I told him about the plaque that we had special made for Bishop. He promptly let me know that was not good enough. So, Ashley and I had to run out and buy the items on the list given to us by Pastor Williams to make a gift basket. I was so resentful that Ashley and I had to run around and buy all of these items with our personal money while the others got the chance to relax. Then, when we presented the gift all of the ladies wanted to step up and take credit as if they had chipped in. This was not the first, and definitely not the last time this happened. I should have left when I had the chance that weekend. It was hard to do because I felt manipulated into staying. Plus, he had professed his love for me. I absolutely didn't want to walk away from that. I wanted so badly to be with him, be a minister, and please God.

2007

Stay or Leave?

We started the year of 2007 with a new building and a few new members. Although it was a storefront, we were all excited to have a building instead of moving from hotel to hotel. We were also enjoying not having to set the church up and take it down every service.

By this time, things between me and Bishop had really cooled off. I am not sure what happened, he suddenly became very distant. He didn't call as much. Also, when we were at church, he only addressed me about things related to ministry. I didn't know what I had done. Then, one day Ashley told me that Bishop had told her that I was not God's will for him. Of course, I was devastated. I was hurt but not surprised that he chose to relay a message to me through Ashley. After all, that's how we started off. So, I pushed my feelings aside and decided to treat him only as my pastor.

A couple of months later, he began pressuring me, Ashley, and Elder Stevens to move to Atlanta. It seemed as if every service he was "prophesying" to the three of us that God wanted us to get to Atlanta as soon as possible. Although I trusted him as my pastor and a prophet, I still didn't have peace about moving. Bishop would put great emphasis on being a prophet and man of God. If we questioned him or didn't comply with his demands, we would be accused of disobeying God by disobeying him as pastor. He would often use the phrases "God told me to tell you," "Thus saith the Lord," and "If I be a man of God" to manipulate us into doing whatever he wanted us to do- even if it went against God. He would manipulate our minds and cause us to second guess every decision. He would cause us to not trust ourselves to make minor daily decisions. Despite having no peace, I went forward with preparing to move to Atlanta. The three of us began to look for jobs and apartments.

During this time, the women problems rose up again in the church. Even though Bishop and I were no longer pursuing a relationship, a couple of the new women looked at me, Sabrina, and Brittany as competition for the spot as the first lady. There was a big mess when two of the women got in a public argument over Bishop. The one that called herself a prophetess had boldly told him what she would do to him sexually. Then, the other one told her that she would fight her, me, and any other woman that would stand in the way of her being with Bishop. All I could do was sit back and laugh. They both ended up leaving the ministry over this incident.

There was definitely a revolving door pattern in our church. Members (mostly women) would join the ministry and a few months later they would be gone. Then, all that would be left was the core group of ministers that were close to Bishop. Some left after being rejected by Bishop. Others left because the drama was too much to handle. The next chain of events caused me to attempt to leave again.

It all started one weekend in February. Ashley and I were on our way to Atlanta as usual. We had plans to meet up with some friends from Huntsville that were going to visit our church. After that, we were going to go to the home of one of the sisters from church that had invited us to stay overnight with her. While we were still on the road, we received a call from Pastor Williams.

"Praise the Lord Minister Tracie. Where are you?" he questioned.

"I'm almost in Atlanta. Is everything okay?" I asked with concern.

He didn't answer my question. He just went right into another question.

"Where are you all staying tonight?" he asked.

"We're staying with Sis. Gloria."

"I don't think that's a good idea," Pastor Williams revealed.

"Why not," I asked him.

He didn't answer me.

"Let me call you back," he said before hanging up on me.

I knew deep down that some drama was about to go down.

Sis. Gloria was a new sister at the church. I had grown close to her, her five-year old daughter, and her cousin who also was a member of our church. Her cousin, Pastor Patterson, had recently been named as a prophetess and eventually second assistant pastor at our church. Sis. Gloria told Ashley and me that she wanted us to start spending the night with her when we came to Atlanta. She said it didn't make sense to keep spending money on hotel rooms when we could just stay with her for free. What she didn't know was that other members had tried to help us as well by offering us a place to stay. Then, Bishop would get mess stirred up between us and whoever was trying to help us. That would result in us going back to getting a hotel room. So, we were reluctant to accept Sis. Gloria's offer.

A little while after my conversation with Pastor Williams, Ashley and I headed to the mall to meet our friends from Huntsville. During dinner, we got on the topic of church. They began to tell us their testimony of escaping from a cult. Ashley and I sat there stunned as they told a story that could have easily been ours. They told us about the control and manipulation that they experienced from the leadership in their church. I pushed away the conflicting thoughts from my mind that drew similarities between their story and what we were going through at our church.

After dinner, we left the mall to head to Sis. Gloria's apartment. I called her to let her know that we were on the way. I didn't get an answer. So, I called Pastor Patterson. There was still no answer. When we got to her apartment, I called again to let her know we were there. I was sent straight to voicemail. A couple of minutes later, Pastor Williams called and said that he and Bishop were in a meeting with Sis. Gloria and Pastor Patterson. He told us that they would call us later. It was almost 9:00 p.m. at this point. We didn't have anywhere to go, so we just sat in front of Sis. Gloria's apartment and waited. A couple of hours later, we still had not heard from them. It was getting late and it was very cold. I called again and was sent to voicemail. I don't remember when, but we fell asleep. Around 2:00 a.m., I woke up stiff and cold from sleeping outside in the car. Ashley was still asleep. I noticed that I had no missed calls, and I didn't see Sis. Gloria's car in the parking lot. I tried to call her again, and it went straight to voicemail. At this point, I felt like crying. I couldn't understand why we had been literally left out in the cold. I finally fell asleep again. When I woke up around 8:00, I decided to call Pastor Patterson when I couldn't get Sis. Gloria. Pastor Patterson answered.

"Good morning. This is Tracie. Are y'all home yet?"

"Yes", she answered with a flat tone.

"Ashley and I have been trying to reach y'all. We slept in your parking lot last night", I said.

"Oh you did?" she asked nonchalantly.

I could not believe how cold she sounded. She was always so sweet. I wasn't familiar with this side of her. It was as if she didn't care that we had slept in the cold. There was no sympathy, compassion, or apology.

"Yes we did", I answered her. "Can we come in and change our clothes?"

"Yes you can come in, but you need to hurry", she commanded.

When we got upstairs, Pastor Patterson let us in. Sis. Gloria didn't even come out of her bedroom to greet us. Her daughter was playing in the living room. I was very close to her little girl. She always ran and gave me a big hug when she saw me. This time she just sat and looked at me sadly.

"Where is my hug?" I asked her.

She still didn't move.

"What's wrong?"

"Bishop and my mom told me I can't talk to you and Ashley anymore," she said sadly. "Bishop told me y'all do bad things together."

I was stunned. That's when I realized that the meeting the night before was about Ashley and me. That's why Sis. Gloria wouldn't let us in her house. Pastor had told her not to. What I wanted to know was what Ashley and I had been accused of. I told Ashley what the little girl had told me. I told her we needed to get dressed quickly and get out of there.

We got dressed and drove to a drug store which was in the building in front of the church. After I parked, I leaned over the steering wheel and cried. I cried from hurt and exhaustion. I was so tired from the night before. Ashley didn't cry though. However, she was angry. We sat in that parking lot and just poured out our hearts. We shared how hurt and disappointed we were with different things that were going on in the ministry.

Finally, Ashley suggested that we just go on back to Huntsville since no one wanted us there. I reminded her that we had friends visiting and we couldn't just leave them hanging. Ashley told me I could go on into the church, but she wasn't dealing with foolishness that day.

Therefore, we rode over to the church. I went in and Ashley stayed in the car. As soon as I walked in the door, I was met with cold stares as everyone went about their duties. I walked in and sat on a row near the back. I wished at that moment I had just taken Ashley's advice and went back to Huntsville.

After about ten minutes Bishop, Pastor Williams, and Pastor Patterson came out of the back office, so we could begin our leadership class.

"Where is Ashley", Bishop asked me as he made his way to the pulpit.

"She's outside in the car."

"Move up to the front", he commanded as he walked away.

He walked up to the pulpit to begin class. I took a deep breath and tried to prepare myself for whatever I was about to face. I knew deep down it wasn't going to be good. He began to address us.

"Praise the Lord saints. I want to talk to you this morning about things that I will and will not tolerate in my ministry. This goes especially for ministers. First of all, I will not tolerate fornication. In case y'all don't know, it is a sin to lay up with somebody you are not married to. Also, being a lesbian is a sin too. Yes, we have lesbians in this church. It's gonna stop today! I will not let anybody up in my pulpit that's a lesbian!"

I could feel the stares on me as I stared straight ahead. I heard the hearty "amens" from the others. I now knew that Ashley and I were being accused of being lesbians. I was surprised that he didn't go ahead and call our names. He loved to humiliate people.

After he spoke, he invited Pastor Patterson to share what she had seen in the spirit. She stood there and claimed to have had a vision of two female members of our church engaged in lesbian activity. She refused to say our names, but everyone knew she was talking about Ashley and me. Tears welled up in my eyes as I listened to a woman whom I loved and respected boldly lie on me and my sister. Then, Pastor Williams got up and alluded to the same thing. He claimed to have had a vision too.

After Pastor Williams spoke, Bishop made an altar call. As he made a call for repentance, everyone stared at me accusingly. Bishop looked straight at me as he made his appeal. I'm not sure why, but I got up and went to the altar. I felt so ashamed, but I had done nothing wrong. I fell at the altar and cried more from hurt than anything. Pastor Patterson came and put her hand on my back. She began to speak in tongues and "rebuke demons" off of me. When I got up from prayer, Bishop handed me the microphone to begin intercessory prayer. I refused it because I knew my spirit was off. During this time, Ashley finally came in. I was glad to see her because I felt so alone. Then, other members and guests began to arrive. They had no idea what had just taken place. We all went on as if nothing had happened. After church, we went out to eat as usual and were a family again. Although that weekend's events were never discussed again, it wasn't the last time Ashley and I would be falsely accused in the ministry.

In March, I made the decision not to move to Atlanta. Although Ashley and I had found an apartment near the church, I still didn't feel peace. Therefore, I let her and Bishop know that I wasn't moving. She took it better than him. He got upset and told me that I was out of God's will. He also told me that I'd better not convince Ashley not to move. I let him know Ashley was a grown woman who could make her own decisions. Despite my reservations, she moved to Atlanta. Not moving worked out for me because in April I got a new job at a car rental company. I was enjoying using my employee discount to rent a car to go back and forth to Atlanta. Then, I could give my car a break from being on the road every weekend.

At this point, the ministers all lived together in an apartment. Around this time, a young girl ran away from home to be with the church. When she left her family, she moved into the apartment with the ministers. Her family had attended our church. When the parents left the ministry, the children kept attending. I would pick them up and take them home each Sunday. Unfortunately, the girl got into a big argument with her parents about the church and decided to leave home for the church. I already thought it was weird that everyone lived together. When she moved in, it got really strange for me. I felt that as a minor she should be home with her family. Bishop thrived on situations like this. He loved bragging about someone leaving their family to follow God. What he really meant was they left their family to follow him. He loved to quote Mark 10:29-30 to encourage us to leave all for God. After much drama concerning her, the girl eventually went back home. She and her brothers then left the church.

During this time, Bishop began to get a lot of out of town preaching engagements. We all would travel with him wherever he went. Any of the members could go but, the ministers and armor bearers were required to go. I loved these trips for two reasons. First, I love to travel. Second, it gave me the opportunity to get hands-on learning from

Bishop. He allowed all the ministers to use our gifts during the revival services. He would let us sing, conduct intercessory prayer, exhort the congregation, and pray for people. We always saw so many miracles in these services. It was during one of these trips that I let my guard down with one of the sisters from the church. Doing so came back to bite me. I mistakenly confided in this sister about my prior relationship with Bishop. The only reason I told her anything was because, she said that he was saying the same things to her that he said to me. I was concerned since she was a baby Christian. I didn't want her to get caught up. She told another woman in the ministry, who also wanted Bishop, what I said. Then, this lady asked Bishop about it. He confronted me about it in front of everybody after a church service. He asked me why I would tell someone that we used to talk when we didn't. I was humiliated that he would sit there and deny everything. Of course, Pastor Williams and Ashley couldn't say anything. They were the only ones that knew the truth. When we got to the restaurant after church, I confronted him. He told me he didn't tell everyone the truth because it wasn't their business what happened between us. I let him know I was upset because it made me look like a liar. That night at evening service, I sat on the front row feeling disgusted with Bishop and the church. I was hurt that he would take away what we had and not even discuss it with me. I was also tired of being manipulated and stressed. I sat there and got angry as I thought of the time and money that I had wasted on him and the ministry. I decided then and there that I was leaving the ministry again.

The week after I decided to leave, my car broke down. I could have rented a car, but decided to use my car as an excuse to stay in Huntsville. After a few weeks, I was off and on with going to Atlanta. This is when Bishop realized that I was trying to leave. He began to work on getting me to stay.

He started with an email. He titled it "God Don't Bless No Mess." He rebuked me in the email over assumptions. He also stated that I was supposed to be living in Atlanta. He warned me not to try and persuade Ashley to leave the ministry. I was so disturbed by the contents of this email that I let my dad read it. He advised me to leave Bishop and the church alone.

In the weeks after receiving the email, I began to receive random calls and texts from members of the church. I knew they weren't checking on me out of concern. If Bishop felt like someone was trying to leave, he would instruct everyone to contact this person. The person would then be told how much they were loved and needed at the church. I was especially suspicious of the phone call that I received from

Ashley telling me that I was missed at church. By this time, Ashley had moved to Atlanta, and we were not on the best terms because of mess that Bishop had stirred up between us. Finally, Bishop texted me saying that I was loved and missed. He also told me that he was not a brainwasher. Even though I felt manipulated by the calls and texts, I still felt guilty for just walking away.

I finally called Bishop before work one morning to let him know that I was officially leaving.

"Bishop, I'm leaving the ministry. This isn't working for me anymore," I told him.

All I heard on the other end was silence.

"Bishop, are you still there?" I asked.

"Yes, I'm here," he said tearfully.

I couldn't believe he was crying. Of course, that made me feel horrible. At the time, I couldn't see that it was manipulation as usual.

"I'm sorry. I didn't mean to upset you," I sobbed.

"It's all good. Do what you gotta do," he said still crying.

He then told me that another sister from the church had called that morning to say that she was leaving too. He then began to apologize to me for being such a horrible pastor. He said I would be better off without him in my life. He laid a major guilt trip on me. I hung up the phone feeling like I was the bad person. This was exactly what he wanted.

After a restless and stressful week of constant calls and pressure, I decided to go back to church. That Saturday, I showed up for a church meeting and let Bishop know I was back. He simply told me to get back in place.

That June, Bishop decided that he wanted to have a Founder's Week. I guess celebrating him once a month wasn't enough. Each night that week would be a church service. That Saturday night would be a formal black and white ball. We had a meeting, so Bishop could tell us exactly how he wanted everything to be. He had every detailed planned. With every event, including his birthday, he maintained control by making the plans and telling us what he required. For Founder's Week, he told us the layout of the program for each night and what he expected us to wear for each service. He even expected us to make sure there were several balloons in the colors he chose floating over him on the ceiling at each of the services.

I remember one day of Founder's Week going to the store to pick up the balloons for one of the services. We had been running errands all day in preparation for the service that night. We had already been there an hour trying to get the balloons blown up. We had about twenty minutes to get across town to the church and not get yelled at for running late. When it was time to pay, one of the brothers from the church wrote a check. I was so nervous because I knew for a fact that he didn't have any money. He didn't have a job at the time. We hurriedly left the store and got in the car. I looked at my phone and saw that we were already a few minutes late. At that moment, Bishop called Ashley demanding to know where we were. She explained that we were leaving the store and headed to the church. He yelled at her and hung up. As I was stressing about what we would face when we arrived at the church, a few of the balloons popped because of the heat. I then leaned over the steering wheel and cried. I was already hot, tired, hungry, and stressed completely out. On top of that, the balloons we had went through so much to get were starting to pop. I couldn't believe we were dealing with all of this madness just because Bishop felt he needed balloons floating over him at church.

Of course he expected us to pay for all of the expenses even though only a couple of us had jobs at that point. I was so tired of us always having to spend money on unnecessary things. We could have been raising money to help others or pay church bills.

In the fall of 2007, we were evicted from our building in Riverdale because we were behind with the rent. We began having church at various hotels again. By this time, membership was up again. By November, we were finally able to move into a new building (storefront) in Fayetteville.

Soon after moving into the new building, Bishop announced that he was being officially elevated to the office of Bishop. He also said that the rest of the ministers were being licensed or ordained in our respective offices. I would be ordained as an evangelist. The two-part service would take place in December. The first night would be Bishop's elevation service. The second would be the licensing and ordaining of the ministers.

The weeks leading up to ordination were very stressful. Everything had to be exactly the way Bishop wanted. This meant everything had to be perfect, or we would be in trouble. The day of the ordination was spent running the armor bearers to every corner of Atlanta to run various errands. As usual, a lot of things had been left to the last minute because none of them had cars. So, I stepped in like always and used my car as a taxicab for my "family". At least a cabby got paid though. I wasn't even offered gas money most of the time. However, everyone knew I would be there for them no matter what.

That night we got back to the church at almost 6:00 p.m. with just enough time to throw our clothes on and get in line for the processional. Bishop wanted the ministers of our church and visiting ministers to march in together wearing clergy shirts and black robes. Once we got to our seats, we all bowed down on one knee together. We stayed that way for a minute or so to give the appearance of praying. Then, we all stood and sat in our seats at the same time. Bishop lived for these kinds of events. I hated the shows we always had to put on just to walk in and be seated. I also hated wearing my clergy collar and robe. It was uncomfortable and didn't make any sense to me.

After the service, which lasted for a few hours, we had a short reception to fellowship with our guests. After that, Bishop told everyone to meet him at IHOP. It was almost 11 p.m. at this point. We were all tired, but we decided to go to eat since Bishop wanted us to. Ashley and Sabrina got in the car with me. When we were almost at the restaurant, we got stopped by a red light. Suddenly, there was a loud sound as our car lurched forward over the traffic line. I looked in the rearview mirror and saw that we had been rear ended. I immediately asked if everyone was okay. Ashley said she was fine. Sabrina was in the back seat crying. She said that her back hurt and she was having trouble moving. I didn't feel anything on impact, but about ten minutes later I began to feel a sharp pain in my neck. The guy that hit us came up to my window and apologized. He let us know that he had called 911. Ashley called Pastor Williams and let him know what happened. He immediately came to the scene of the accident to check on us. Sabrina and I ended up going to the ER where we spent hours. They finally released me to go after I was told that I had a neck sprain.

I spent the next afternoon running last minute errands and picking people up for the ordination services, even though I was in pain from the accident. Bishop still expected me to help the guys unload the heavy equipment for service. He got upset and called me lazy when I couldn't help due to my injury. Despite everything that happened, I was ordained as an evangelist that evening.

We closed out the year at the Fayetteville building. Although we still had our building, we lost more members. Once again, drama in the ministry ran people off. A couple of women left due to Bishop's rejection though. The revolving door continued to turn. And... the drama continued to build.

2008

Making Moves

By March of 2008, we had been evicted from the Fayetteville building. As a result, we went back to going from hotel to hotel. A lot of times we didn't know until Sunday morning where we would be worshipping. It was such an ordeal driving around to first find somewhere that would let us have services. Then, we would have to make a couple of trips in my car and Bishop's car to get all of the equipment to wherever church would be that day. Then, another sister and I would have to go pick everyone up. We were also in debt to a few hotels because sometimes we did not have enough money to pay for the room.

It was around this time that God laid it on my heart to start my women's ministry Beauty for Ashes. Beauty for Ashes was designed to minister through conferences and outreach services. I began to plan for my ministry launch which would be a women's conference in Huntsville. At first, everyone in the ministry was very supportive. Then, all of a sudden, things changed.

It all started when I asked my dad to teach at the morning session of the conference. I wanted to get a male perspective. This made Bishop mad and jealous. He said that since he was my pastor, he should have been asked to teach. He told me that I should never have an event and not ask my pastor to be involved. I guess I missed that *particular* scripture in the Bible. Anyway, he and I had a big argument about it on the phone. After we hung up, he had Ashley call me to tell me how wrong and disrespectful I was for not inviting him to preach. It wasn't anything personal against him. God just had not led me to ask him to participate in the service.

In the weeks leading up to the conference there was much conflict between him, the other members, and me concerning the conference. The others sided with him, of course. However, Pastor expected us all to be in agreement with him, even if he was wrong. After that, I made sure to always invite him to participate in whatever I was doing. I would even invite him to have words if I was preaching at another church. Sometimes he would preach another sermon behind mine. He had a way of taking over other people's services. He would be asked to give a couple minutes of encouraging words but would end up preaching, prophesying, and laying hands.

Around May, Bishop called us together to have a meeting at his apartment. He let us know that God had led him to move to Huntsville where he would open a new church. I told later that he allegedly left Atlanta due to some criminal activity that caught up with him. Bishop also said that he wanted everyone to move to Huntsville with him to start the new work. At this point, we were down to eight people. All of us were ministers except one. The sister that was not a minister decided not to move because she was expecting a baby and wanted to stay close to her baby's father. Everyone else agreed to move. I had mixed emotions about the announcement. On one hand, I was glad that I wouldn't have to drive to Atlanta anymore. On the other hand, I knew more would be required of me with Bishop being in the same city. I knew he would expect to have all of my free time just like he did with the others.

In June, Bishop and the other members moved to Huntsville. At first, everyone stayed in a hotel together. After a few weeks, Bishop and Pastor Williams found an apartment. The other four ministers got an apartment together. We then moved into our new church which was another storefront building.

Just as I feared, Bishop expected so much more from me. Every day after work, he wanted me to come wherever they were that day and hang out or run errands. We also spent time walking around knocking on doors to invite people to church. We also went to various parking lots and put fliers on cars. We did this sometimes for hours. After every church service on Wednesday and Sunday, we all went out to eat together like we did in Atlanta. Sometimes we would be at a restaurant until 6:00 in the morning. It was hard to maintain this schedule because I had to be at work every day at 8:00 a.m. I also lived with my parents at this time. I didn't want to disturb them by coming home in the middle of the night. Bishop expected us to eat out every time we were together. He would be so offended if you said no. Sometimes we couldn't afford to go and would be forced to go anyway. We would have to sit there and watch everyone else eat. One night, he forced Ashley to go even though he knew she didn't have any money. We were all seated and eating when Pastor Williams turned his attention to Ashley.

"Are you hungry?" Pastor Williams asked her.

"No sir. I'm fine," Ashley answered. We could tell she was lying.

"Stop lying. You know you're hungry. Eat this," Pastor Williams said throwing a packet of saltine crackers at her that had come with his chili. He and Bishop then burst out laughing.

Sadly, we all laughed along with them. We didn't want it to turn on one of us. Sometimes Bishop and Pastor Williams treated us like dogs. However, we were expected to do whatever we could for them if they were in need. Bishop would pay for us to eat sometimes if we didn't have the money. However, he would make us feel guilty about him paying for us. Plus, he would throw it in our face later during an argument that he had done something for us.

Bishop also expected me to go "gleaning" with the other ministers. Gleaning was an activity in the ministry that I truly hated. Bishop called it gleaning, but it was nothing more than begging. It was his way of raising funds for the ministry. He actually considered it a form of witnessing. I felt that if it were witnessing then the gospel would be shared. I would have even accepted going out to invite people to our church. I could not understand why we invited people to church only to turn around and ask them for money. I don't recall the disciples standing on the side of the road begging. They were too busy preaching the gospel. I never felt comfortable with gleaning. Thankfully, I never had to participate in it because I lived in Huntsville. But when the church moved to Huntsville, my first thought was that I didn't want to walk around with a bucket hustling people out of their money. I say hustling because taped on the side of the bucket was a list of things that the money went towards. Some things on the list didn't even exist. For example, a church daycare and a food pantry were nonexistent items on the list.

Anyway, the time came when I was asked to go glean. I met the other ministers in front of a local grocery store. Bishop and Pastor were not there. They rarely participated in fundraising activities. They usually came at the end to collect the money. I was so mad that I had to be there. I listened as Sabrina explained to me how gleaning worked. I was told to stop people going in and out of the store, invite them to our church, and then ask for a donation. I decided that I would invite people to church but not ask for money. I did not want someone's first impression of the church to be us asking them for something. To make it look like I was collecting money, I separated from the group and slipped a few dollars from my purse into the bucket. About an hour into gleaning, Bishop and Pastor Williams stopped by to see how much we had collected. They took the money that we had raised up until that point. It felt like we were being pimped. They then told us to go to another store and glean for another hour or so. When we got to that store, we spent most of our time there dodging security. It was illegal for us to walk around the parking lot asking for money. I decided that after that evening I would never glean again. At that point, I didn't even care if Bishop went off on me.

The next time the ministers went out to glean, I didn't show up. I called Bishop and let him know that I wasn't gleaning anymore. He was very upset at hearing that. He was most upset that I had asked the advice of my dad and another pastor before coming to him. After that, we had a church meeting about it. He was still upset, but thankfully he agreed that I didn't have to glean anymore.

Not long after that meeting, Pastor Williams called me in the middle of the night.

"Praise the Lord Evangelist Tracie. The ministers are going out to glean tomorrow around 5. Can you meet them to help?" he asked.

"Bishop said I that I didn't have to glean anymore," I responded.

"You just don't understand what gleaning is biblically. You should check out The Great Harvest website to get more information," he recommended.

"Actually, I have been on that site. What they do is totally different. They actually feed people like in the Bible," I replied.

When I said that, he began to yell at me.

"You need to lower your voice! I will not be disrespected!"

I hadn't even raised my voice during our conversation. I was still half asleep! Then, I heard Bishop yelling in the background. That's when I realized why Pastor Williams was yelling. He wanted Bishop to think that I was disrespecting him so I would get in trouble. The next thing I knew, Bishop was on the phone going off on me. I was so hurt and confused. All I wanted to do was sleep and they were on my phone with foolishness. However, I never gleaned again.

After a few months of being in Huntsville, the church was growing. We began to get a lot of students from a local college. We all traveled with Bishop every time he went out of town. We continued to see mighty miracles while out on the road. The only part that I didn't like was that Bishop would rent vehicles from me through the rental company I worked for. He would sometimes turn cars back in with no gas and an unpaid bill. I would have to cover his expenses out of my own pocket.

Around this time, we also got a few older ladies in the church. Bishop liked them being in the church because they all had good paying jobs. He loved when people with a lot of money joined. Of course, like in the past, a couple of these women wanted Bishop. They felt like they could buy him. He would let women spend money on him knowing they had no chance of being with him.

One thing I was glad about was that Bishop and I were repairing our friendship. It felt good to be close to him again. This time we were strictly friends except for the few times that he asked if I still had feelings for him. Of course, I still had a lot of love for him. I even wondered if we might end up together. Every now and then we would have the "what if" conversations. I would go back and forth between wanting to be with him and being over it altogether. But, at the end of the day, he was my pastor and friend. We would sit up at night and talk for hours. He was close with the other members as well. That's why we were so loyal to him. No matter what he did or asked us to do, we had his back because of what he meant to us. He would talk us through problems, encourage us, and keep us laughing. He believed in us and our ministries. That made it so hard to leave when we should have.

Although things were looking up for the ministry, there was still some trouble. It began with the ministers losing a couple of apartments. Ashley moved back in with her family. The other ministers moved from hotel to hotel. The first incident happened when they were arrested for not paying their hotel bill. They were in jail about a week. We had to scramble and raise money to bail them out. I felt so bad that they had been arrested. I knew how much they had struggled since arriving in Huntsville. From this moment on, some ministers of the church kept getting into more trouble. Each time was worse than the last. It was bad for all of us whether we were involved or not.

The next thing that happened directly affected me which was my fault. Brittany got arrested at a grocery store one night for writing a bad check. This affected me because at the time of her arrest she was driving a car from the rental company where I worked. I was the one that had rented the car to her. When the fleet manager got a call that the car was in impound, he traced the rental back to me. I was looked at in suspicion because I had rented to her without her using a debit or credit card which was a requirement. I had also waived the underage driver's fee and given her my employee discount. I was called into my manager's office.

"Do you know this person?" he asked while showing me the rental agreement.

"Yes. She is my god sister," I answered trying to play it cool.

He then informed me that she was in jail for writing bad checks and the car was impounded.

"Did you know that she has been writing bad checks?" he asked me.

"No didn't," I answered truthfully.

I had no idea she had been writing bad checks. I later found out she was put up to it by Bishop. I recall a couple of the ministers writing checks everywhere we went while running errands and traveling. I assumed they had the money since they were working at that point.

My manager ended up reprimanding me for giving her the discounts and then gave me her belongings that had been left in the car. From that point on, I feel as if my managers were concerned and suspicious about me having ties to people involved in criminal activity. I didn't realize the full extent of what some of the members were involved in.

By the time I got back to my desk, I had many missed calls from church members wanting to know what had happened. They had seen Brittany's mug shot on the news. I didn't tell anyone that I knew anything. I wanted to talk to Bishop first to see what I was allowed to tell. During my time with the church, I became a pro at answering people's questions without answering them. I always kept things vague to cover and protect Bishop and the church. He coached us on what to say and what not to say. When I finally talked to him, he was mad and confessed how Brittany had made the ministry look bad. It was crazy how he was the mastermind behind the bad things that happened but did not take any responsibility. If anyone got caught doing something wrong, he would place the blame on that person. I saw him more than once leave a person hanging out on a limb alone after asking them to do something wrong.

Shortly after the check writing incident, Brittany was put out of the church in the middle of the night. We had just come back from hosting a powerful revival service in Memphis. Everything seemed fine when we left Memphis. However, while on the road, there was tension between her and Bishop. I remember them texting each other and looking upset in the car. By the time we got back to the church, Bishop was telling Brittany that she needed to leave and never come back. I don't remember what he was mad at her about. It was probably a minor issue that he had made into a major one. I do remember that she didn't have anywhere to go nor did she have a car. She had been staying with one of the other ministers, but Bishop told her that she couldn't go over there anymore. We all watched helplessly as she grabbed her belongings and started walking down the road. Bishop then let us know that she was disfellowshipped again. This wasn't the first time that this had happened to her. When people were disfellowshipped, we were not allowed to have any communication with them. It would be as if the person died or never existed. Weirdly enough, Bishop could stay in contact with them though. He always referred to those that left as the "bastards" of our church since they didn't have him as a father anymore.

About a half hour after she left, we drove up the road coming back from dropping off the rental car. It was around two in the morning at this point. Pastor Williams was on the phone with Bishop dogging Brittany out. All of a sudden, I spotted her walking on the side of the road. Pastor Williams saw her too and told Bishop she was wandering around on the side of the road. They both started laughing and making jokes about her as Pastor Williams drove right past her. I couldn't believe how cruel they were being to her. Brittany went on to have a rough few weeks on the streets. She was even hospitalized for stress- related sickness. A few weeks later, Bishop let her return after she stood up in front of the church and repented for her sins.

Despite the trouble, the church continued to grow. We soon needed a bigger building. Bishop and all the ministers found a building and agreed that it would be perfect for our church. It was an old warehouse, but it had plenty of room. We were concerned about how high the rent was, but we trusted that God would provide the finances.

We moved into the new building in August, and God continued to add people to the church. He even added a couple of new ministers. We experienced tremendous growth spiritually as well. We would have Holy Ghost blowout services every time we came to church. We continued to see mighty miracles done by God through Bishop, our ministry team, and the lay members. I loved that Bishop encouraged everyone whether they were a licensed minister or not to walk in the gifts and power of the Holy Spirit. We also had great fellowship with other local ministries that were similar to ours. One particular alliance ended up getting us back on the news though.

The next incident involved Bishop, Pastor Williams, a few of the ministers, and another local minister named Minister Brown. I didn't know all of the details, but I did notice when things began to unravel.

It all started one Wednesday night in October during bible study. Bishop was preaching when we heard tires screeching in the parking lot. We saw someone drive up almost on two wheels. Then, the door flung open. Minister Brown, who we had always enjoyed regular fellowship with, stormed in.

"Praise the Lord Evangelist", he spat out as he strode passed me and up the aisle.

He plopped down in a front row seat and stared daggers at Bishop until he finished preaching. After service, they went in Bishop's office. They stayed in there for almost an hour. When they came out, they both looked stressed.

A week later, I spent the day trying to get in touch with Bishop and some of the other ministers. I could not get anyone on the phone. When I arrived at church that night for bible study, no one had arrived yet which was not usual. Usually the armor bearers would be there early setting up Bishop's towels, water, etc. An elderly lady from our church, Mother Green, was with me. She and I went in to begin intercessory prayer. About fifteen minutes later, other members began to show up. When Pastor Williams finally showed up, Bishop was not with him. After I finished praying, Pastor Williams took the microphone. He informed everyone that we would not be having bible study that night. We would have a few minutes of prayer and go home. Pastor Williams was just letting us know that Bishop was under the weather when five cops and a K-9 dog walked in the church. They blocked the front door as they lined up across it. The one female cop stepped forward and addressed Pastor Williams.

"Sir, are you Alan Williams?" she asked to confirm his identity.

"Yes I am." he answered. "Could we have a minute to close out in prayer?"

"Sure, but make it quick." she replied.

After we prayed, Pastor Williams dismissed us. When he came down from the pulpit, he pulled me to the side.

"I'm about to get arrested. I need you to get everyone out and lock the church up. Then, call Bishop for further instructions."

We were all quiet and shaken as we prepared to leave. We watched as one of the cops took the police dog walking around the building to sniff everything. To this day, I don't know what that dog was looking for.

After the others left, I locked up and walked out to my car with Mother Green. That's when we saw Pastor Williams being arrested. I hurriedly got Mother Green inside the car. I then stood outside the car and called Bishop. I fell apart when I heard his voice.

"The cops just got Pastor Williams!" I screamed into the phone.

I was frantic and crying by this time. I told him about the cops and dog coming into the church.

"Calm down so I can tell you what's going on." he beckoned. "I'm not sick. I'm hiding out from the cops. I knew they were coming tonight. They already got the others." he said referring to some of the other ministers.

He then let me know that he planned to turn himself in the next day. He told me that Minister Brown had gotten them caught up in a theft ring. Bishop said they were just trying to earn extra money and had no idea what they were really getting into. I found out later that Bishop knew exactly what was going on but ended up getting everyone else caught up.

I stood there holding back tears as Bishop gave me instructions on what to do the next couple of days and who to call to try to get the others out of jail. He said that his parents would get him out the next day.

"I need you to be strong for me these next few days. It will be rough, but God will bring us through it." he promised.

"Yes sir." I responded tearfully.

"Now take Mother Green home and get some rest. Good night."

"Good night Bishop."

I numbly got in the car. Mother Green was frantic and wanting to know what was going on. I knew I wasn't released to tell her the whole truth. I just told her that Bishop was sick and the police were just picking on Pastor Williams. I told her it was a big misunderstanding. Mother Green then began to pray. I just sat there thinking about all that had taken place that evening. I never thought that I would see a police dog in church or someone getting arrested there. It was just way too much for me to digest.

The following days after Pastor Williams was arrested were very stressful. Although Bishop turned himself in, his parents were able to get him right out. The others remained in jail. I had called those whom I was instructed to call, including some of the members. No one had any extra money to help. Then, I was told to ask Mother Green if she would put her house up for bond. She refused. When I told Bishop, he made me keep pressuring her. I felt so bad because I didn't want her caught up in any of it. Finally, he left her alone about it.

A couple of weeks after that, I closed on my first home. Immediately, Bishop pressured me to put my house up for bond.

Like Mother Green, I refused to do that. It was just too risky. Of course, Bishop was upset that I wouldn't do it. He accused me of being selfish as usual. Then, he told me that I thought I was better than everybody else because I bought a house. He had the nerve to tell me that I shouldn't have bought a house because he didn't have one.

"Why would God bless you with a house before he would bless your pastor with one? That doesn't make any sense," he bitterly told me one day.

What he was saying didn't make any sense. He was weird about things like that though. If one of us got a blessing, he would initially be happy. He would even share our testimony or ask us to share it during church service. Then, along the way he would get mad and bitter about someone else being blessed. The following year when he finally moved into a rental home instead of an apartment, he promptly rubbed it in my face.

"You ain't the only one in the church with a house now," he boasted when he moved in.

Towards the end of November, those that were in jail were released. The father of one of the members paid the bail for Pastor Williams and a minister named Brian. Brittany and Sabrina were released into the custody of their families. This meant they each had to move back to their hometowns in order to remain out of jail. Bishop was really upset at Brittany. He told us that he heard that she was dogging him and the ministry while she was in jail. She probably just took off the rose-colored glasses she had been wearing while being strung along by Bishop. Bishop was also upset that Sabrina had to leave. They had been close friends for a long time. He called me one evening and asked me if I could meet with her and convince her to stay in Huntsville. Since he was too much of a coward to face her family, he asked me to do it. This was his normal routine. I agreed to meet with her, but personally I was happy for both of them. I was glad that they had an opportunity to walk away from the madness and be with their families again.

The night I met with Sabrina, I took one of the other members with me for support. We all decided to meet at Burger King.

We walked into to the restaurant and headed over to the table where Sabrina was sitting with her grandmother and her grandmother's pastor who both greeted us warmly. We had fellowshipped with them when our church was still in Atlanta. We then sat, and I began to explain why we were meeting with her.

"Please don't leave," I begged. "I don't want you to get out of God's will. God has been using you so mightily in the ministry. Don't you know how much we love you? Don't you know how much Bishop loves you? He wants you to stay."

I pulled everything out of my hat to say in order to get her to stay. We all used the same script when trying to convince someone not to leave. Everything that I was saying was true, but I only said it because I knew it would please Bishop if I could convince her to stay.

While we were talking, Bishop called and asked me what was going on. I told him that we were still talking to her.

"Tell her I said don't go!" he demanded.

So, I told her what he said.

"Y'all just don't understand," she said while beginning to cry. "I don't have a choice. I have to stay in my grandma's custody to stay out of jail."

Suddenly her grandmother jumped into the conversation.

"Y'all need to leave her alone and let her go back to Atlanta. It's Bishop Davis' fault that she went to jail anyway. He knows, and she knows it."

Although I didn't know the full truth yet about what happened, I believed what she was saying about Bishop. However, my loyalty was with him, so I had to defend him no matter what.

"You don't even know what you're talking about. You need to keep your mouth off of my pastor!" I snapped.

I felt bad about speaking to her grandmother that way, but Bishop was still on the phone. I wanted him to hear me defending him, so I wouldn't be accused of not doing it later. Her grandmother and I continued to argue back and forth. Finally, her grandmother stood and began to make gestures like she wanted to fight.

"Come on then! You wanna fight? Bring it on!" she yelled.

I then stood to my feet.

"What's up then? What you wanna do?!" I yelled back.

We were yelling at each other when her pastor jumped up and stood between us.

"Y'all can't do this. Just stop it!" he exclaimed trying to get us to calm down.

That's when I stopped yelling and looked around. Everyone in the restaurant was staring at us with horrified looks on their faces. I was beyond embarrassed that I had just threatened to fight someone's grandmother in the middle of a restaurant. This was a lady that had always been nice and encouraging to me. I knew I needed to get out of there.

"Let's go," I said to the sister that had come with me as I grabbed my belongings. She stood to follow me.

I turned back around to hug Sabrina and let her know I would be praying for her. We both had tears in our eyes. Then, we turned and walked out of the restaurant. When we got in the car, I put the phone to my ear. Bishop was still there. I could hear him loudly laughing.

"Hey. I'm back," I said still stunned about what had just happened.

"Oh my God!" he exclaimed while still laughing. "I can't believe you almost fought her grandma! I guess you really do love your pastor and your church. Thanks for standing up for me and having my back."

I couldn't believe he was laughing. Although I was disturbed by the whole situation, I was glad that he was pleased with me. A couple of years later, I had the opportunity to apologize to Sabrina's grandmother for disrespecting her. She told me she had already forgiven me because she knew we were all under Bishop's influence.

The next disturbing thing that occurred was because of more bad decisions made by Bishop. He had a bad habit of not paying the musicians sometimes. I feel like he thought he could get away with this because a lot of the musicians in Huntsville were his friends. We went through changes in musicians the way we did with members. It was a revolving door. Everything came to a head late one night after we returned from conducting revival services in Memphis. We were unloading our luggage from the van when two cars came speeding up in the parking lot. The cars screeched to a halt a few feet away from us. Two of our musicians and the ladies that they were with at the time jumped out of the car. One of the musicians was smiling but had a look in his eyes like he was about to do something crazy. The other musician just stared menacingly at Bishop.

"Good evening saints", the smiling musician said sarcastically. "Let's all go inside the church. We need to talk about our money."

I felt so uneasy. I knew both of the musicians and considered them to be good guys. But, I couldn't shake the bad feeling that I had. The musician who was staring at Bishop finally spoke up.

"We came to get our money. You owe us and you need to pay us for today too. How you gonna call us at the last minute and say you're not having church Kerry?" he asked addressing Bishop by his first name.

"You will respect Bishop Davis", said Pastor Williams while stepping forward. Bishop and Pastor Williams were all about titles. Bishop even corrected his oldest and closest friends when they addressed him by his first name.

"Shut up, Alan!" the musician shouted while addressing Pastor Williams by his first name as well. "This is between me and him."

The other musician then spoke up. He explained that they were there because Bishop owed them a couple of weeks' worth of pay. They also wanted to be paid for that day because they were notified at the last minute that we were staying another day in Memphis. I know because I am the one who was told to call them Sunday morning a couple of hours before services would have started. Bishop knew the evening before that we were staying an extra day. He should have told them then.

During the whole exchange, Bishop never said a word. He stood against the wall and remained silent. He, along with the rest of us, watched while Pastor Williams and the musicians argued back and forth. He once again let someone else fight his battle.

"What happened to you, Kerry?" one of the musicians asked Bishop. "We used to be so cool. You not the same since you been back. We don't talk or hang like we used to. All you want to do is be around Alan."

The rest of us stood there stunned. I secretly enjoyed seeing someone stand up to Bishop and Pastor Williams. In my book, they deserved to be on the receiving in of being told off for once.

Finally, Bishop stepped forward and told Pastor Williams to give them the money. Pastor Williams rolled his eyes as he pulled a wad of cash from his pocket. He gave some money to one of them. Meanwhile, the other musician was walking out of the door with our drum set. He told Bishop he was holding on to it until he got paid. I found out later from another one of our musicians that one of the guys who came to get the money had a gun on them that night and was prepared to use it if they weren't paid. I don't know if that was true, but that may explain the bad feeling that I had.

We were soon evicted from our building. We moved around to different hotels for the rest of the year. We had no idea we were getting ready to face another big trial.

2009
Change is Coming

The year started with us moving into a new building. We found another storefront church near my house. We were seeing growth in the ministry again. More students from the local college were coming. God was using a lot of these kids in mighty ways. One of them, Keith, became especially close to me. He reminded me of a younger version of Bishop because of the way God used him to preach, sing, and prophesy. He was like a little brother to me.

It was around this time that Brian, who was also like a younger brother, and I moved into my new house. He had just lost his apartment and had nowhere to go. So, Bishop asked if Brian could move in with me. So, we moved in and didn't have anything. We didn't even have blinds in the windows or a refrigerator. All we had was faith. By now we were both unemployed. I had been laid off from my job with the rental company. When I got laid off, Pastor told the other ministers that I deserved it for thinking I was better than everybody.

It was during this period when I discovered how twisted the relationship between Brian and Bishop was. Since Brian was an armor bearer, he was required to accompany Bishop everywhere. Brian and Pastor Williams were on call 24/7. That's how Brian lost his job once. He had to quit the job because his shift coincided with an out-of-town revival. It seemed like Brian was in trouble all of the time with Bishop. Most of the rebuking sessions were aimed at Brian. A couple of times, we were all called to meet Bishop in the middle of the night because he and Brian had a disagreement. He would call us to come pray the "demons" out of Brian. I remember waking up sometimes and hearing Brian in his room crying on the phone. I could hear Bishop yelling through the phone. This would go on for hours.

"Bishop, I repent to you. Please forgive me," he would beg.

Also, Bishop would test Brian's loyalty constantly. Bishop called me one morning and told me that he was going to tell Brian that he had been in a bad car accident just to see how he responded. He was satisfied when Brian got hysterical after hearing about the fictional accident. I felt so sorry for him. He tested us all in different ways, but I feel that Pastor Williams and Brian got it the worst.

Things in the ministry went on as usual. It was always a roller coaster. We would have tremendous highs and then things would drop low. The ministers walked around on eggshells most of the time because, Bishop's abuse was usually reserved for the ministers that were the closest to him.

One day towards the end of January, Bishop called all of the ministers into a meeting. We were told that we were having another ordination service in February. Bishop told us he was being elevated to the office of an apostle. Pastor Williams and I would be installed as a bishop and second assistant pastor respectively. I never felt called to a pastoral office, but I went along with what Bishop wanted as usual. All the other ministers were being licensed as ministers. Bishop's mother, Mother Davis, was being ordained as an evangelist. Also, Ashley was being ordained as a prophetess. He let us know that there were certain clergy items that we needed in order to be ordained. He told us that if any of the items were missing, we would not be ordained. One of the items that he said we needed was new ministerial robes. He said that the ones Elder Stevens made for us in Atlanta looked cheap and homemade. I thought the robes that she made looked very professional, but I stayed quiet to keep peace. We all glanced around nervously. All of us were unemployed except one minister. The robe alone would be a couple hundred dollars. We had no idea how we would get extra money to buy these items.

With only a few weeks to prepare, one of the ministers and I decided to go to the local Christian stores to see if we qualified for charge accounts. We were declined at one store, but were able to open an account at another store. When it was time to put the names of the authorized users on the account, I didn't feel comfortable putting my name down. I told the minister whom I was with that I would figure out a way to pay for everything. So, she only put her name down at that time. Later that night, I told Keith about the account.

"This isn't going to work out. Just watch. It's going to backfire," he asserted.

By the next week, I had my other items for ordination. I still didn't have my robe though. I went to the minister with the account and asked her if she could order my robe for me and I would pay her back. While we were at the store placing the order, the lady at the register asked the minister if she was Bishop. She thought Bishop was a woman because his name sounded feminine to her. I thought that it was strange that Bishop's name was on the account. I also noticed that the church name listed on the account was another local church instead of ours. As usual, I kept my mouth shut, even though I knew something wasn't right.

Meanwhile, a couple of weeks after that, the ordination ceremony took place. I felt like the money that we spent was such a waste. As usual, the ceremony was hours long and a big show. I was so glad when the whole ordeal was over. What we all didn't realize was that we were experiencing the calm before the storm.

Surprisingly, I was now an assistant pastor at the church. However, it was an awkward position. Although I had some of the same privileges as Bishop and Pastor Williams, I still was not quite equal to them. I would be lying though if I said I didn't enjoy eating at the head table instead of serving at it. I also enjoyed having doors held for me instead of holding doors for grown men. I had been battling arrogance since I joined the ministry due to Bishop breeding competition between the women by puffing me up. Moving into this new position didn't help that. The gap between me and the other women was wider than it had ever been. I also had new duties. It was my job each week to find a place for us to have church once we were evicted from our building. I would call hotel after hotel to see if we could have service. Also, every Saturday night, I was responsible for calling each member to see if they would be attending church the next day. If I didn't get an answer, I was instructed to "blow their phone up" until I got an answer. Once I got a *yes* or *no,* I had to report back to Bishop who was coming, who wasn't, and why the person that said no wasn't coming. Then, I would have to call those that said they weren't coming again and try to convince them to come to church. Once, a sister couldn't make it to church because back pain had her bedridden. Bishop told me to step outside during service to call and tell her that she needed to come to church. He said if she didn't get out of the bed and come, that meant she didn't have enough faith that God could heal her. He was very upset when she still would not come.

A few weeks after the ordination, I was at home relaxing and watching TV. Usually, Brian and I would sit up and watch a movie, but he was staying at Bishop's apartment that night. Since he was gone, I decided to go to bed. I was headed to my room to get in the bed when my phone started ringing.

"She got us in trouble! The police looking for us and we on the news!" Bishop exclaimed frantically.

"What", I asked in disbelief.

"I need you to get over to my apartment ASAP! We're about to have a meeting with all the saints."

"Yes sir," I said before hanging up.

I numbly stumbled to my room to change out of my nightclothes. I couldn't believe that members of the church were on the news again for criminal activity. My heart sank as I thought about family and friends seeing mug shots of fellow church members, including my pastor, again. I felt sick to my stomach. It had only been a few months since the last time members of my church were in jail.

What happened this time? I wondered as I sped across town to Bishop's apartment.

When I arrived, the other members were arriving as well. After we all got seated, Bishop explained what happened. He explained how they had been on the news because they were being charged with theft from the store where the minister set up the charge account. He told us that the minister had made the account under another church's name, charged a lot of things, and didn't pay. He also said that she added him and Pastor Williams to the account without their knowledge. That's why there was a warrant for their arrest as well. After hearing that information, everyone was in an uproar. I sat there praising God that I didn't put my name on the account. Finally, someone suggested that we all walk over to this minister's apartment and confront her. She lived directly across the street with her family. Of course, Bishop and Pastor Williams were all for it.

Therefore, we all walked across the street to go off on the minister. It was about 20 of us. Of course, her family looked puzzled that we were there, for it was extremely late at night. We had a heated discussion that escalated when we found out that she had already turned herself in and gotten bailed out. This made Bishop angrier because, he felt like she got him in trouble and left him hanging. This apparently made everyone else angry.

"You better watch your back. I'm gonna kill you", said one of the male members jumping to his feet.

Things just got out of control. We all yelled at her and accused her. Bishop and Pastor Williams just sat back and enjoyed the show. They even laughed when the minister was threatened with physical harm. Finally, it all came to an end when her mother told us it was time for us to go.

The next few days were trying. At Bishop's instruction, we all continued to harass the minister by calls and text messages. We completely shunned her in person. One night when she came to prayer, no one would even come inside the church until she left. Everyone just sat in the parking lot. I was the only one inside with her and I refused to speak to her because of my loyalty to Bishop. The Sunday that she decided to return to church, Bishop made her first sit and listen while his parents and a visiting minister rebuked her. She then had to stand up and publicly repent to the church for her actions. Then, Bishop let her know that she was being sat down from all of her duties in the church. During this time, Bishop and Pastor Williams turned themselves in.

Once again, Bishop's parents got him out. Bishop asked me to sign to get Pastor Williams out. I didn't feel comfortable, but I was told that I could sign for him without paying anything or involving my home. The bondsman said that all Pastor Williams had to do was pay him back in installments and make sure he appeared in court. So, I signed for Pastor Williams and thought that was the end of it. I was completely wrong.

I found out later that this particular incident of theft was once again Bishop's fault. He was the mastermind as usual. I found out that he asked the minister to add his and Pastor Williams' name to the account. I noticed that Bishop had new items from this particular store all of a sudden. He even gave us gifts from there. I often wondered where he was getting the money for these expensive items because he couldn't even pay his own bills. Neither he nor Pastor Williams had a job. They often relied on me or other members to take care of their bills along with our own. Anyway, they were the ones that charged so much that it drew attention to the account. The other church that was listed on the account noticed fraudulent activity on its account and reported it. There had been a mistake made with the accounts by the store. Instead of admitting the mistake, they put the blame on those listed on our account. When the store contacted the members of our church for payments, Bishop wrote a bad check. It turned out that the investigators had been looking for Bishop, Pastor Williams, and Sabrina over past fraud and theft. Over the next year, the minister who opened the account continued to take the blame for something that she was instructed by Bishop to do. When I found out the truth about what really happened, I felt so bad about how we treated our sister.

Anytime anybody did anything wrong or was accused of doing wrong, the whole church developed a mob mentality against them. Bishop himself orchestrated these attacks. He really thrived on drama. For instance, he would sit on the phone with different members of the church and gossip about other members. If you wouldn't talk about somebody, you would be accused of being too deep and to lighten up. If you responded just to please Bishop, he would then run and tell that person what you said about them. He would never tell what he said or that he started the discussion. He would dog people out for how they looked, what kind of car they drove, how much money they had, their spiritual gifts, etc. Then when that person confronted you, Bishop would leave you out on the limb alone. He would lie to cover himself or expect us to lie to cover him. He always threw rocks and hid his hand. He would also get us to tell on each other. He would pester you until you told him what you knew about members of the church. He used this information sometimes in sermons to expose the sins of members. He could not be trusted with private information. If you confided something to him, you could just be sure that the whole church would know. He would use things against me from my past that I confided in him from when we first met. We had young men at our church that had confided to Bishop that they struggled with homosexuality in the past. Along with discussing these admissions during sermons, he would publicly refer to those struggling as having faggot spirits. He also told me in great detail things about these guys' private lives. I knew so much about every single person in the ministry because of him. I'm sure he told all of my business to others as well. Along with the messiness, Bishop began to get even more controlling. He continued to dictate our every move, what we wore, where we went to eat, etc. He definitely didn't like us hanging with people outside of the church. I had to downplay the few outside friendships I had so that Bishop wouldn't become suspicious. If I hung out with someone else, he would call and text me the whole time. Although my friends were Christians, he would warn me not to fall into sin with them because they weren't members of our church.

Bishop didn't even like us hanging out with other church members without him. I remember one incident in particular. That day started like any other day. All of our plans were laid to the side to be at Bishop's beck and call. Ashley, Brian, Keith, and I met that morning at the church for prayer. Bishop and Pastor Williams came as well. After prayer, the ministers hung around as usual until we were released. Keith and I just sat and talked while Ashley and Brian cleaned up Bishop's office since they were armor bearers. Finally, Bishop came out of his office around four o'clock.

"What are y'all about to do?" he asked me as he walked into the sanctuary.

"I'm not sure yet. I gotta talk to everybody else," I answered.

"Well, I'm about to go run some errands with Pastor Williams. I'll talk to y'all later," he said.

After that, we all walked Bishop and Pastor Williams to their car and said good bye. Then, the four of us got in my car. I was surprised that Bishop hadn't asked Ashley and Brian to go with him since they were usually on duty. We all weren't sure what to do since we weren't used to having free time. We then decided to go get something to eat because it had been hours since we all had eaten breakfast.

When we arrived at a local pizza place, we were all laughing and talking. We were all enjoying our moment of freedom. We went in, fixed our plates at the buffet bar, and sat down to eat. As soon as we sat down, my cell phone rang. Fear paralyzed me as the Caller ID showed that it was Bishop calling. I didn't want to answer and have him find out that we were eating without him. I also didn't want to be rebuked for ignoring his call. I decided to just answer. Either way, we were in trouble.

"Hello," I answered.

"What are you doing?" he asked.

"'I'm eating with Ashley, Brian, and Keith," I replied nervously.

"What?! Oh so y'all just go out to eat and don't think to invite your pastor," he said his voice rising in anger.

"Bishop, it's not like that. We just...

"Wow...put me on speaker phone!" he ordered cutting me off.

"Yes sir," I said. "Y'all it's Bishop. He wants to say something to all of us."

Everyone had a look of dread on their faces. I then let Bishop know that I had him on speaker phone.

"Can y'all hear me?" he asked.

"Yes sir," we responded in unison.

"I'm just trying to figure out why y'all out eating and didn't think to invite me or Pastor Williams. How y'all just gonna go behind our backs and plan an outing? I invite y'all to go everywhere with me, but y'all don't give me the same respect."

We sat there silently as he went off on us for what felt like an hour but was really a few minutes. I was so embarrassed because others sitting near us could hear the way he was addressing us. Finally, he told us to enjoy our meal and our evening. He then promptly hung up without even giving us a chance to respond. Nobody said it, but we were all wondering if we would have to hear about this incident again at church the following Sunday. Thankfully, we didn't.

Around April, I began to plan the next Beauty for Ashes Conference. A few weeks prior, I met a local minister named Min. Clark. She showed up at our church one Sunday to visit. Bishop asked her to come have words and let God have His way. I really admired the way she prayed and prophesied under the anointing. Following the service, I asked her if she could speak at my upcoming conference. She immediately agreed be the speaker. Over the following weeks, she and I became very close. We spoke on the phone daily. I enjoyed talking to her because the conversations were spiritual. She didn't talk about people or stir up drama. I remember once she invited me to her home for lunch. I sat down at the table to eat, and I felt like crying. I was so overwhelmed by the peace that I felt in her home. I was always so tense and stressed trying to make sure I did and said the right things at all times. Trying to be perfect is exhausting. But, perfection is what Bishop demanded. We all lived in constant fear of losing our salvation because of how Bishop taught us. He loved to tell us that we were going to "bust hell wide open". There was never any grace.

Anyway, I remember Min. Clark telling me to sit and let her serve me my lunch. I wasn't used to being treated this kindly. While we ate and talked, my phone began to ring. It was Bishop of course. I surprised myself when I just let it go to voicemail. I didn't want to have to tell him that I was at Min. Clark's home. I also knew that whatever he was calling about was probably negative. At that moment, I just didn't want to hear it. Min. Clark noticed the look on my face when he called.

"You're tired aren't you?" she asked.

"Yes," I answered as I began to cry.

Before I could stop myself, I began to tell her some things about the ministry that were bothering me and hurting me. Then, she prayed for me. I left her house feeling strengthened. On the way home, I called Bishop back to see what he needed. I reluctantly let him know that I had been at Min. Clark's. He was not happy about that. He didn't know that she and I had grown so close. He immediately began to work at tearing apart our friendship. He began to tear down this lady whom he at one time spoke so highly of. He finally forced me to replace her as one of my conference speakers. He threatened that he would not participate in my conference if she did. I knew that if he didn't participate, I would never hear the end of it. It was so painful to have to tell Min. Clark that I didn't need her to participate in the conference anymore. She said she understood, but I know it hurt her feelings. God had probably revealed to her what was really going on. After that, our friendship was never the same. We gradually talked less and less. Finally, we weren't talking at all.

It was during this period that Bishop began to tear down the good relationship that I had with Brian too. He couldn't stand how close we had become after he moved in with me. Every day he would call me to gossip about Brian. Then, he would turn around and call him to do the same to me. He sowed so much discord between us, we began to not trust each other and treat each other differently.

One Friday morning, Bishop sent out a text to all of the members saying that his light bill needed to be paid. This was his personal light bill at his apartment. Since he didn't work, he mainly depended on others to pay his bills. At this point, I was paying the bills at my home and helping with his expenses with the unemployment I received. Brian did what he could to help me. He wasn't working either. Anyway, this text came right when I was trying to figure out a way to keep our lights from being turned off. Although I really didn't have it to spare, I knew I had to give something to avoid being rebuked for not giving. When I arrived at the church, there were members lined up outside the door to give Pastor Williams money. Once I gave my money, I went back home to try and figure out what I could do to keep my lights on. I called Brian to see if he could contribute anything. When he didn't answer the phone, I decided to text him about our light situation. I didn't get a response. About thirty minutes later, I heard a car pull up in the driveway. I looked out the door and saw that it was Bishop and Pastor Williams dropping Brian off. I waved at them. Neither one of them waved back. They just looked at me like I was a stranger.

What have I done wrong now? I thought.

I noticed Brian wasn't getting out of the car. That's when I received a text from Bishop wanting to know why I asked Brian to help me with my light bill when his still wasn't paid. He called me selfish for asking Brian to help me. He accused me of wanting him to sit in the dark while I enjoyed having lights. He claimed that I didn't care about him at all. I texted him back that I was sorry for offending him. At that point Brian came inside.

"I don't have any extra money to put towards our bill. I'm gonna help Bishop pay his," Brian informed me.

"That's fine." I said feeling exhausted by the whole situation.

I couldn't believe that Brian was going to leave me hanging. At the same time though, I understood why he chose to do what he did. I'm sure he had pressure from Bishop to help him instead of me. Thankfully, I received some unexpected help that allowed me to keep my lights from getting turned off.

It seemed like I couldn't ever do anything right or please Bishop. We all lived in fear and anxiety. You never knew if something you said or did would tick him off. If anyone offended Bishop, we would have these rebuking sessions where the person in trouble would be rebuked publicly. These sessions sometimes lasted for hours as Bishop would rehash everything that the person had ever done wrong in front of all the other ministers. Sometimes, it would be in front of other church members. One night, we were in a meeting like this from 7:00 p.m. until 6:00 a.m. the next morning. There were mixed emotions about these meetings. Although we would feel bad for the person in trouble, we would be thanking God that it wasn't us that time. We usually didn't know beforehand who was in trouble when we were summoned to these sessions. Bishop would only let us know the time and place. It was usually at his place or the church. On the way to the meeting, I would feel so sick. I would rack my brain trying to recall if there was anything that I may have done to make Bishop mad. Sometimes we would show up, and it would simply be a church business meeting.

One particular rebuking session really stands out concerning me. Bishop texted me early one morning and asked if I could come to his house around noon so we could talk. I said sure. I didn't think anything of it because he didn't say it was a meeting. When I pulled up in the driveway, I was surprised to see the car of one of the ministers parked in front of the house. When I walked in the door, several pairs of eyes were on me. There was Bishop, Pastor Williams, Ashley, Brian, one of the ministers, her kids, and grandkids. I looked around the room, smiled, and greeted everyone.

"Praise the Lord!" I said cheerfully.

All that I received in return were blank stares and silence. I immediately felt sick as I realized that Pastor had set me up. This meeting would be on me, but I had no idea what I had done wrong. I walked over to the couch where Ashley was sitting and sat down next to her. She wouldn't even look at me. By now, Ashley and I had a very strained relationship. We were cordial, but the closeness we had was long gone due to Bishop's messiness.

After a few awkward minutes, Bishop called the meeting to order. He promptly let me know that I had offended everyone in the room with my recent actions. He explained that each person was going to tell me how I offended them. I sat there numbly as each person said how they felt. As usual, I was accused of being selfish and mean. I was told that I thought I was better than everyone else in the ministry. I will admit that I was arrogant at times due to being put on a pedestal by Bishop. He would always give me compliments about how I dressed, carried myself, or even ministered. He would compare us all to each other. He did this especially with the female ministers. Unsurprisingly, they resented that. On the flip side, he would also dog me out to the other women as well. To protect myself, I put distance between me and the other members. I was scared to be close to anyone in the church. It always backfired on me because Bishop would come in between us. Anyway, when it was Bishop's turn to speak he went all the way back to the first time I tried to leave during his installation as pastor. From there, he brought up incident after incident where he felt like I let everybody down. After everyone was finished, I was given a chance to respond. I knew from previous experience that nothing that I said at this point would be received.

"I repent for offending you all." I responded tearfully. "It wasn't my intention to hurt any of you. It won't happen again."

"You don't mean that," said Bishop accusingly. "You are so arrogant, and your spirit is off."

I apologized again. This time my apology was received as good enough. After they attacked me for over an hour, the meeting was interrupted when a bounty hunter knocked at the door. He was there to pick up Brian because he had missed a court date and failed to pay the bail bondsman. Guess who had to give the bounty hunter money to go away? That's right. The same person that they had just roasted for being selfish and uncaring was the same one they asked to help Brian out. After the bounty hunter left, the meeting then turned on Brian. Bishop got mad at him for not being grateful that I had just kept Brian from going to jail. Brian didn't even say thank you to me. As a result, the next hour was spent listening to Bishop tell Brian that he was selfish, treated people like garbage, and always expected others to bail him out of trouble that he brought on himself. I was so glad the heat was off of me.

Shortly after this, it was time for the Beauty for Ashes conference. I didn't have a key to the church, so I had to wait for Pastor Williams to show up and let me in. About thirty minutes after the service was supposed to start, Pastor Williams showed up and let me know that we weren't going to be able to get in the church. We were behind on rent as usual and the landlord wouldn't let us in until we paid what we owed. He had changed the lock on the door, so we couldn't get in. I was beyond embarrassed. I had a parking lot full of women waiting to get in. I had to cancel that evening's service. I then called a pastor I knew and asked her if I could use her building for the next night. Thankfully, she said yes. I then had to walk around to each car and explain that due to unforeseen circumstances, that night's service was cancelled. I then let each lady know where the conference would be the next night.

The next afternoon as I was studying my sermon for service that evening, I received a text from Bishop. He wanted me to meet Pastor Williams and a locksmith at the church. He wanted to get a new lock, so that we could get in on Sunday and have service. That would have been fine if it wasn't wrong. As I mentioned before, the landlord had the locks changed because rent hadn't been paid. Of course, Bishop expected me to pay the locksmith out of my pocket. So, we met the locksmith at the church. He didn't ask any questions. He just changed the lock and took the money from me. I was so scared that the whole thing would come back and bite us. It didn't though. However, the power had been turned off at the church, so we couldn't have service there anyway.

That evening, we had the next service of the conference. After that service, Bishop let me know that the final night of the conference would be held at the church of a pastor that we fellowshipped with. This pastor was one of the few that we fellowshipped with that wasn't shady. Bishop preached at this last service. After the backlash that I received for the previous conference, I made sure to give him space to preach. At the end of the service I took the offering money to the back to count it, so I could pay Bishop and the musicians. The offering ended up not being enough to pay everyone. I decided to go ahead and pay the musicians. I didn't want any more run-ins with them. I then pulled Bishop to the side and let him know I would meet him with his money the next day. I told him I had to wait until the bank was open, so I could get the money. He told me that was fine. I couldn't really tell if he was upset or not. He seemed like he wasn't, but sometimes I just didn't know. By the time I got to my car, I knew for sure that he was upset. As I walked to my car, I noticed that everyone from our church was gathered around him. They were trying to decide where to go eat. Nobody even acknowledged me to see if I wanted to go. Out of desperation, I asked Bishop if I could speak to him.

"What's going on?" he asked coolly.

"I just wanted to take care of your dinner tonight," I said pulling a ten dollar bill from my purse. It was my gas money. It was all the cash that I had on me, but I would have given him anything just to make sure he wasn't mad at me.

"Oh ok...thanks," he said as he took the money from my hand and turned away from me without another word. As I closed my car door, I overheard him tell the other members to meet him at Denny's. I cried all of the way home.

The next day, I called Bishop a few times, so we could meet up. He wouldn't answer his phone. I couldn't understand why he was upset. It's not like I was trying to skip out on paying him. I just didn't have the money on me the night before. It wasn't my fault that there wasn't enough in the offering to pay everyone at the same time. Later that afternoon, Mother Davis called me.

"Praise the Lord Pastor Winn. This is Evangelist Davis. Do you have few minutes to talk to me?" she asked.

"Yes ma'am." I replied. I knew she was calling on behalf of Bishop. I took a deep breath and prepared for whatever was about to be said.

"I would just like to explain something to you," she started. "When you have any type of program, you not only invite your pastor to preach, you make sure they are paid before anyone else."

She then began to tell a story about how she took care of her old pastor no matter what. She talked about always putting the "man of God" before anyone, so that you will be blessed. Finally, she let me know that Bishop was really upset and disappointed that I chose to give him his money the following day instead of the same night of the service. He was also mad that I had chosen to pay for his dinner instead of giving him all of his money.

"I just didn't want any trouble from the musicians. They get very mad when they're not paid." I explained to her.

She wasn't there the night the musicians confronted Bishop so she didn't understand my concern. I then let her know that I had been trying to reach Bishop all day in order to give him the money. She then told me that once we hung up, I needed to try to call him again. That time he answered.

I then met him and gave him his money. I decided then and there that I was done with conferences for awhile. They were too stressful and always got me in some sort of trouble.

The next evening, we all met at the church late at night to move our things out. We had to move in the dark since the power was still out. Some of us had flashlights or the lights on our cell phones to see. Of course, Bishop didn't come, even though he orchestrated the move. Instead of paying our rent, he decided we should just move out without saying anything to the landlord.

For the next couple of months, we had church in hotels and Bishop's apartment. Speaking of apartments, Bishop changed apartments as much as we changed churches. Bishop told us that three months is the longest you can go without paying rent. This meant if we had a building, we expected to be there three months. The same went with Bishop's apartments.

This particular summer was spent trying to find a new church building, traveling with Bishop, and having fundraiser car washes. I absolutely hated the car washes. The members of the church would get to the car wash location early in the morning to set up. Ashley and I would stand on the side of the road in the hot sun with car wash signs for hours. Everyone else would wash cars. We only got a couple of breaks to get something to drink or go to the bathroom. We couldn't stop until Bishop showed up and said we could. As with gleaning, Bishop and Pastor Williams would show up to collect the money at the end. Sometimes, Pastor Williams would come early and help wash the cars. If Bishop came early, he would sit inside and watch us work. No matter how much money we brought in, there would be none when it was time to travel. I honestly didn't know where all the money we raised went.

One of the most memorable car washes was the result of a build-up of events. It all started when Brian got a call from Bishop early one Friday. Bishop wanted Brian and Ashley to clean his parent's house in Muscle Shoals. Neither one of them had a car, so Pastor told them to get me to bring them. I let them know that I didn't have enough gas to take them that far and back. We were all still unemployed and struggling financially. Of course, neither of them offered gas money. Bishop called me greedy and selfish for asking for help with gas. That's something that was beginning to take a toll on me. Everyone in the ministry dogged me out constantly but would call me for help as soon as they needed something. I was so tired of being used. Even though we were always together (and sometimes having a good time), I felt disconnected from everyone else. Anyway, Ashley was able to get some money from her mom, and we prepared to get on the road. Before we could leave Huntsville, Bishop called to say that a member's husband had died. He instructed us to meet him at the sister's house to comfort her and her family.

When we got to the family's house I sat on the floor near Bishop because there were no more seats. Of course the same grown men we held doors for didn't bother to offer their seats. I sat there silent and mad. I felt guilty for being upset during the family's time of mourning, but I was just tired. I was exhausted in my mind, body, and spirit. I felt disgusted as I looked around at all of us ministers dressed alike. We all had on head to toe black in the middle of summer. As usual, Ashley and I had on stockings along with all of those hot black clothes.

While we were there, Bishop told me to go buy chicken for everyone with my own money. Nobody offered to help me pay for it. I simply said "yes sir," and left to get it.

After leaving the family, we went to the Country Inn and Suites to look at a meeting space for church. Everyone just sat around in the lobby while I booked the room. When we were in the parking lot preparing to leave, Bishop mentioned that his parent's house still needed to be cleaned. He asked me if I wanted to come eat with them in Muscle Shoals. I knew the only reason that he invited me was to make sure Brian and Ashley had a way home. I promptly let him know that I was tired and going home. I then sped out of the parking lot. Immediately, Bishop began to call my phone. I kept sending him to voicemail. He sent me a text message. I ignored it. I knew that I was in trouble, but I didn't care one bit. After getting something to eat, I went to my parent's house to talk to my dad. Of course, he encouraged me to leave the church. But, I didn't want to leave until I knew for sure it was God's will. I was so scared of making a wrong decision. I was so scared of making decisions about anything on my own since Bishop always told me what to do. Later that night, I finally called Bishop back. I poured out my heart to him about how I felt about everything. I let him know I was burned out and tired of being mistreated. He assured me that he loved me and was for me. I felt peace when we hung up.

The next morning, I got up to prepare for the car wash. I felt so much dread and depression that I called Mother Davis and asked for prayer. After she prayed, she asked if I was okay because I didn't seem to be the day before. I truthfully told her that I felt burned out and left it at that. About an hour into the car wash, I got a call from Bishop.

"Why you calling my momma with mess about the church?!"

I was stunned. In our conversation, I didn't even mention the church.

"Bishop, I didn't say anything to your mom about the church. I only asked her for prayer, and I told her I was feeling burned out."

"I'll talk to you later," he said before hanging up on me.

When Bishop arrived several hours later, he instructed everyone to come inside the restaurant except me. I could see through the window that everyone was looking at me. They did not look happy. Finally Pastor Williams came out and told me I could come in. As soon as I sat down, Bishop began to rebuke me for asking his mom for prayer. He also let me know he was disappointed that I confided to him about feeling used. I sat there in disbelief as he rehashed our private conversation in public. I was humiliated. I tried to apologize, but he kept cutting me off.

"I guess I will just stop pastoring since I'm a horrible pastor that makes people feel burned out. As a matter of fact don't even celebrate me for Father's Day tomorrow. I'm not a good father anyway."

He did this constantly. He would make remarks to make us feel guilty and win our sympathy. He used this tactic to manipulate us into feeling we were wrong instead of him.

When he told us not to bother celebrating Father's Day, everyone went into an uproar.

"Thanks a lot Tracie. You just ruined Father's Day. Now, I can't celebrate my dad because of you," said Ashley referring to Pastor. She then jumped up and ran to the bathroom crying.

Only one sister showed me some compassion. She came over and put her arms around me. I held on to her and cried.

"It's okay," she said. "Just let it out."

"Don't coddle that demon of confusion in her." Bishop commanded.

That sister ignored him and just kept her arms around me. I was so grateful for her kindness. A few minutes later, Bishop jumped up and decided he was ready to leave. Everyone got up and followed him to the parking lot. I was standing there trying to figure out what to say to make things better when I saw Bishop fall to the ground. Pastor Williams and Brian tried to get him up, but he was out. The next thing I know, an ambulance pulled up and got him. I remember being pushed into one of the minister's cars and being told we were headed to the hospital. After all that had happened,

I was surprised they wanted me to go with them. We sat in the waiting room for hours. Nobody was speaking to me still. Finally Pastor Williams came out and let us know that Bishop had a diabetic episode and passed out.

"Something stressed him out," said Pastor Williams looking directly at me.

I felt horrible. Bishop had been in bad health for years because of diabetes. He was constantly sick. He spent a lot of time going in and out of the hospital. Only those closest to him knew how sick he really was. He would still preach and sing as if he felt fine. I genuinely admired how he always pressed his way.

The next day in church, I publicly repented to him and everyone else. I was then accepted again. Then, it was business as usual.

That summer we continued to have church in Bishop's apartment and hotels as we looked for a new place. During this time, members began to drop like flies. One young lady pulled me to the side one day and asked what a cult was. I told her about Jim Jones and Jonestown.

"Are we a cult?" she asked. "My parents said that we are. They want me to leave the church."

"No sweetie. We're not a cult." I responded. "We are a real church that teaches the truth of God's Word. And we're submitted fully to our pastors because the Bible says we should be. We follow them as they follow Christ."

I rambled on with more things that I had been programmed to say. I had asked myself many times if I was in a cult. I kept convincing myself that I was not and everything was as it should be. Shortly after this conversation, the young lady's parent's made her leave the church. She was one of several college students who belonged to the church. Bishop loved bringing in people that were young and naive. He also recruited those from dysfunctional backgrounds.

After the young lady left, many of the other students began to leave. They complained about Bishop being in their business all of the time and trying to control every aspect of their lives. One young minister told him specifically when he left that Bishop should just preach the Word and let us choose to apply it or not. Bishop would hound us with calls and texts to make sure we were doing right at all times. He told us who we could and couldn't hang around. He told us where we could and couldn't go.

Finally, Keith was the last of that group to leave. The night he came back from summer break, he had a new car and a new attitude. That night as he gave me and Brian a ride home from Bishop's apartment, we laughed and talked as usual. But, something was different with Keith. Later that night, Bishop sent me a text that said Keith had quit the church. I immediately called Bishop.

"Can you believe this negro left us?" Pastor asked as he answered the phone.

"What happened?" I asked.

"He called me after y'all left and told me: "I can no longer meet your demands. He must be crazy! Nobody has made any demands of him. I didn't hold a gun to his head and make him do anything," Bishop refuted.

I couldn't believe how in denial Bishop was about his controlling ways. I knew personally that Keith's academics had suffered from being part of the ministry. As a minister and armor bearer he was always on call. He couldn't get study time in and sometimes missed class. His grades had slipped. He decided to leave the church and focus on school which was his reason for being in Huntsville in the first place.

After Keith left, there were just a few of us left. Bishop called a meeting in August to let us know he had found a building and he was changing the church name. He claimed God told him to change the name. I always felt like he changed it because of all the negativity associated with our church. He also told us he was changing some of the positions in the church. I was replaced by Mother Davis as Second Assistant Pastor. I was now an evangelist again which was fine with me. That was my true calling and assignment.

We moved into the new building, which had been a radio station, in August. We started to grow again. Another crop of college students joined the ministry after being invited by the only college student that we had left. We all were really struggling during this time. Bishop and Pastor Williams had lost another apartment. I was still unemployed and now without a car. The other ministers were in the same situation. Bishop often told us when we went through that it was due to hidden sin in our lives. If he went through it, he said it was an attack of the devil or a test. He had a lot of hidden mess but loved to expose others, even though he was struggling with the same things.

For a few weeks after being evicted, Bishop and Pastor Williams stayed in a hotel or at Bishop's parent's home. They finally found an apartment. As usual the ministers and armor bearers were expected to move everything, put it away, and clean up. Moving Bishop was always an all-day affair. We even had to move him in the middle of the night a couple of times with no light because the power was off. When he moved into this place, I knew he expected us to be there. So, I drove my car although my dad had told me not to drive it that day because it was having problems. I picked Ashley up and we headed to Bishop's new apartment. On the way we pulled over to a store to buy Bishop some drinks and my car quit. We immediately called Bishop to tell him what happened. Then I called AAA. About ten minutes later, Pastor Williams pulled up and told us he was there to pick up Ashley. Bishop wanted to make sure she still came to clean the apartment. My heart sank as I watched them pull away leaving me to wait for help alone. It felt as if I was totally worthless if I couldn't do something for somebody. This wasn't the first or last time that I was stranded, sometimes alone, on the side of the road trying to do something for the church. I didn't dare tell my parents how my church family treated me most of the time. They already had major concerns about the ministry anyway.

After Bishop got settled into his new place, he called a meeting with the ministers. He introduced the new church by-laws. Some of things in the new by-laws were unbelievable. The very first thing at the top of the front page stated that Bishop was the "Head N***a In Charge" and the "Set Man of the House". It also said that as the evangelist of the house I was to recruit souls to the ministry each week to get acquainted with Bishop's voice. I felt like people should have been there to get acquainted with the voice of God. There were also rules for the armor bearers. They were required to accompany Bishop everywhere that he went and not to speak unless spoken to. It also outlined the items that the armor bearers were to carry each place for Bishop. The by-laws also outlined how the women could not wear pants and female leaders must wear stockings at all times. It said men could not wear girly hairstyles. According to the by-laws, neither men nor women could look like a h*e. It also stated that I was responsible for making sure people got to church and "blowing up their phones" to follow up with them. And when calling anyone, as usual, there was a script to follow as if I was a telemarketer. Another thing that really stood out to me was the chain of command/order of succession/dissolution of the church. Bishop had very specific instructions on how things were to be if he died or the church closed for good. The by-laws stated that if Bishop died, then Pastor Williams would be the pastor. Mother Davis would then be the assistant pastor. I had never seen anything like this.

Around September, I reconnected with a relative of mine. She tearfully told me one night about the things going on at the church she attended. I didn't tell her that her church sounded a lot like mine. Instead, I invited her to our church.

Since I was in charge of our witnessing (aka recruiting) team, I was under so much pressure from Bishop to bring people in all the time. I was always so torn about it. I wanted to please him, but I didn't want others to get caught up in any mess. Sadly, I still didn't have the courage to leave myself. After a couple of weeks of visiting, this relative joined our church. Her daughter joined soon after. Immediately, Bishop began to work on sowing discord between me and her daughter. He kept up mess back and forth between us. It's sad that neither one of us realized the common denominator was him whenever there was confusion between us.

One evening in mid-October, Brian and I were out running errands for Bishop when we got a frantic call from him.

"Somebody broke in the church and tore everything up!" he shouted. "Y'all get over here now!"

We sped over to the church. When we got there, the first thing we saw was the shattered glass door. We also saw that there were open spaces where the glass windows once were. We stepped inside the door to find that someone had trashed the sanctuary. Chairs were knocked over. Banners were on the ground. The potted plants were all knocked down and scattered around. We were then summoned to Bishop's office.

"Can y'all believe this?" he asked as we came in his office. "The devil is really busy. He just doesn't want to see us go forward in the Lord. Anyway, I need y'all to call the police. When they get here, y'all talk to to them and fill out the report. I'm going to stay in my office. Don't tell them I'm back here because they might try to harass me. The police always try to bother me because of the call on my life."

When the police arrived, the first thing they asked was if Bishop was there. I lied and said no to cover him. I told them that we were there alone just in case they tried to bother Pastor Williams too. After we filled out the report, the police left. Then, we began the clean up process with a couple of the members whom Bishop had called to come help. We never found out who vandalized our church. I do know that Bishop definitely had enemies though.

The next month, things went from bad to worse. Pastor Williams missed a court date and refused to make payments to the bail bondsman. There was now a warrant for his arrest. Since I had signed his bond, I was being held responsible for the money. I did have a new job at the time, but I didn't have enough after bills to pay the bondsman. I was upset that he would even put me in that position. The bondsman called me every day and bounty hunters began coming by my home looking for Pastor Williams. I was stressed and scared because the bondsman was threatening to garnish my wages. He even confronted me and Pastor Williams at the jail one night when we were down there bailing Brian out again. Each time I spoke to Pastor Williams about it, he was nonchalant. He said that he would call the bondsman but never did. Whenever the bondsman asked where Pastor Williams was or if I had seen him, I lied and covered for him.

Everything finally came to a head on the evening of our church Christmas dinner at Ryan's. There was no drama that night. Everyone was eating and having a great time. We were all laughing and talking when I got a call from my dad.

"Hey Dad." I answered.

"Hey" he replied. "Where are you?"

"I'm at Ryan's eating with the saints."

"Which Ryan's?"

"The one down South." I said referring to the location on the south side of town.

"Okay," he said. "Well, I'll talk to you later. Bye."

"Okay. Bye."

About twenty minutes later, the two bounty hunters I saw outside my home came walking into the back dining area where we were seated.

"Is there an Alan Williams here?" one of them asked.

"I'm Alan." Pastor Williams answered turning in his seat.

"You need to come with us. There's a warrant for your arrest," he said pulling Pastor Williams up from the chair just as he was putting some butter on his cornbread.

"Can I finish my cornbread?" Pastor Williams asked as handcuffs were placed around his wrists.

"No sir," the man answered roughly.

"Tracie, take my wallet out of my pocket. I'm gonna call y'all as soon as I can."

I reached in Pastor William's pocket and took his wallet out. They then turned Pastor Williams around, walked him through the restaurant in handcuffs, and took him out the door. We all sat there stunned. We then gathered our things and rushed out of the restaurant. Once we got outside, I pulled Bishop to side to talk to him.

"Bishop those were the bounty hunters that have been coming to my house. They have been calling me for weeks about Pastor Williams."

"Wow," Bishop replied. "We all need to go to my apartment and figure out how we're gonna get him out of jail."

"Yes sir." I said.

Bishop then told everyone to follow him to his apartment. On the way there, my dad called me again.

"Tracie, where are you?" he asked.

"I'm on my way to Bishop's apartment. They just came and got Pastor Williams out of Ryan's and took him to jail." I answered frantically.

"You need to come home," my dad said.

"I can't come home right now. I have to go to Bishop's. He asked everyone to come over." I said.

Then my mom got on the phone.

"Tracie, you need to come home. Your dad is not feeling well," she confirmed.

I was so torn. I needed to go check on my dad, but I didn't want to be in trouble with Bishop. I decided to go home. I was actually relieved that I didn't have to sit up all night and look for bail bondsmen and call around asking people for money. As I pulled up to Bishop's apartment, I called him on my cell phone.

"Bishop, I need to go check on my parents. My dad is sick." I told him.

"That's fine," said Bishop assured. "I pray that he's okay."

"Thank you Bishop. Please keep me posted about Pastor Williams." I said.

"I will. Talk to you later," he replied.

"Ok. Bye." I reassured.

When I got to my parent's house, I went to their bedroom and found my dad lying across the bed. My mom was sitting on the edge of the bed. They both looked traumatized.

"What's wrong Dad?" I asked.

"After you left to go eat, the police showed up over here," he said sitting up. "They said they were looking for you. When I looked outside police cars were out there. The police explained to me that you were affiliated with some criminals that they have been looking for. They showed us mug shots of Bishop and Pastor Williams. They told us that they had a warrant for Pastor William's arrest but would take you in if they couldn't find Pastor Williams. They said they could do this because you signed his bond. Well, I told them they weren't taking you anywhere and that I would help them find them. That's why I called and asked where you were. The police were standing right there. Then, I had them follow me down to Ryan's, and I pointed out everybody's car. Then, we came back home."

After my dad finished telling me what happened, I leaned against the door frame for support. I couldn't believe how close I had come to going to jail over church foolishness.

"Tracie, you have got to get away from these people. They don't care about you. They are just using you," my dad begged.

I confessed, "I'm ready to leave them alone. I'm so tired of this mess."

I was so disturbed by the events of that night, I decided to just spend the night at my parent's house. As I was getting ready for bed, I received calls from Brian and Ashley going off on me about leaving. They also claimed that I got Pastor Williams caught up.

"I can't believe this!" Ashley exclaimed. "You got Pastor Williams in trouble and then you left!"

"I didn't tell the police where Pastor Williams was. The police came to my parent's house and threatened to take me in if they couldn't find Pastor Williams. I almost went to jail!"

"The police weren't really gonna take you in!" she snapped. They were just trying to scare you."

She said a few more things about me not being loyal to our pastors and the church. Then, she hung up on me. Then, Brian called.

"I can't believe you did this. You're gonna reap what you've sown," Brian told me before hanging up on me.

I felt so discouraged that I just went to bed. I put my phone on silent just to get some peace and relief. When I woke up the next morning, I had numerous missed calls and text messages from Bishop, Pastor Williams, Brian, and

Ashley. I had a three-page long text from Pastor Williams saying that I set him up and that God was going to get me for betraying him. He even said that the bondsman told him that I gave him up to the police. That was an outright lie. There was a long text from Bishop going off on me as well. Bishop and Pastor Williams both stated in their texts that I should have covered the men of God no matter what. They always expected others to take the fall for them. That's the same mentality that got everyone locked up all of the other times. They were trying to protect Bishop. Then, there were voicemails from Brian and Ashley wanting their belongings that they had left in my car the night before. I didn't have the energy or desire to deal with any of that first thing in the morning. I decided to call Bishop later that day and let him know I was done with them and the church.

I finally got enough nerve that afternoon to call Bishop. I was so nervous about how he would respond to me after the events the night before.

"Praise the Lord Bishop." I said when he answered the phone.

"Praise the Lord Evangelist." he responded with a sarcastic emphasis on evangelist.

"I just wanted to repent to you about what happened last night. I'm sorry for leaving y'all last night. I just wanted to make sure my dad was okay." I said.

"I understand." Bishop said coolly. "We all called you and texted you last night. You wouldn't even answer or respond."

"I didn't hear my phone. I had it on silent." I explained.

"Oh. So you purposely didn't want to hear from us?" he asked.

"Brian and Ashley had called going off on me and I just wanted peace." I admitted.

"Oh okay." Bishop uttered.

"Bishop, I also wanted to say that last night really hurt. I almost got locked up because of Pastor Williams. He's trying to act like he's the victim, but he is the one that missed his court date and didn't make his payments," I refuted. "I've been begging him for weeks to contact the bondsman to make a payment arrangement. He wouldn't do it. Anyway, I'm tired of all of this. I feel like it's time for me to just move on. I can't do this anymore."

"Tracie, I don't want you to leave. We don't want you to leave. Last night everybody was emotional, and it just got out of hand. I'm so sorry that all of this happened to you," he apologized while changing his tone.

I couldn't believe he apologized. He never apologized for anything. When things happened we always had to repent to him even if he was the one that was wrong. That was the only way we resolved issues. We had to seek his forgiveness.

"I receive your apology, but I still want to go." I responded.

"Let me tell you what happened after you left and see if you feel differently," he pleaded. "After you left, Brian and Ashley came in to tell me that you left without saying anything. I let them know that you had called me and I released you to go. Then, they got mad and started saying that you should have stayed since you were the one that got Pastor Williams locked up. When they said that, one of the sisters got on the phone and started calling up people to go to your house and beat you up. Then my dad spoke up and told everybody that they should be mad at the minister that got him in trouble in the first place."

He was referring to the fraud and theft incident with the Christian bookstore. Bishop then told me that all of the anger shifted from me to her. Mother Davis got on the phone and told me how much I was loved and needed at the ministry.

"See," Bishop proved after getting back on the phone. "Nobody's mad. We all love you and want you to stay."

Once again, I decided to stay. My parents were very disappointed but let me make my own decision.

So, I immediately went back into the routine of being at Bishop's beck and call. One thing that did change during this time was the way I felt about him. I loved him, but I decided once and for all that I did not want to be with Bishop. I was tired of being strung along by him. I vowed to treat him as my pastor only. Because of his insecurities, he had a hard time with rejection. He would try to have the "what if" conversations or send me pictures of him flexing in his tank top. He would get so mad when I would shut it all down and tell him it wasn't like that with us and to stop being inappropriate. He didn't like anybody whom he had feelings for to move on. For example, he got really mad when Brittany decided to get married to someone else. He didn't want us but didn't want anyone else to have us.

2010
Time to Say Goodbye

We began 2010 surprisingly in our same church building. At this time, there was an unusual peace. Everyone was getting along. The drama seemed to have died down. However, it was far from over. Bishop began to really come down hard on me, Ashley, and Brian for every little thing. It got so bad for Ashley that she became suicidal.

One morning before church started, she wrote a note to Bishop stating that she was tired and didn't want to live anymore. It was a clear cry for help. Instead of being sympathetic and praying for her, Bishop read the note out loud at the beginning of service. He mocked her for being weak and told her if she wanted to kill herself to go ahead and do it. We all sat in stunned silence. Ashley just sat in her seat and stared sadly at the floor. Later on in the service, Bishop called all the ministers up to pray with her and rebuke the spirit of suicide off of her. He then hugged and encouraged her. You never knew what you were going to get with him.

My turn came one night when I was called into Pastor Williams' office after a Sunday night church service. I nervously followed Pastor Williams to his office. I hadn't been in trouble since the Ryan's incident. I had no idea what I had done this time. When I stepped into his office, Bishop and Mother Davis were already in there. I can't remember what I got in trouble for that time, but I do remember Bishop going off on me. After he finished yelling at me, I simply responded with "that's fine" instead of "yes sir" or "I repent to you". I just didn't care at that point. After I responded, he suddenly sat up in his chair.

"I'm not scared of you Tracie Winn! I'm tired of your attitude and your mess!" he yelled.

Then, he threw his phone at me. It landed at my feet and broke into a few pieces.

"Look what you made me do!" he yelled as Pastor Williams scrambled to pick up the pieces.

I stood there stunned. I had witnessed him throw and break many things. However, this was my first time being on the receiving end. On top of that, I couldn't believe he had the nerve to blame me because he couldn't control his temper. To try and restore peace, I apologized for making him angry.

Then, Pastor Williams spoke up all of a sudden and told me that he forgave me for calling the cops on him. He said the Lord had let him know that I turned him in, but he decided not to hold it against me. I explained to him once again that I lied for weeks to the people that were looking for him to cover him and that my parents led the cops to him that night.

"You don't have to keep lying," he responded. "I know the truth and I forgive you."

I couldn't believe he would sit up and lie on God like that. He also still refused to take any responsibility for what happened. If he hadn't committed a crime in the first place, none of that would have happened to him.

Then, they accused me of trying to take over the church. Bishop said that Ashley had told him that I told her to remove Pastor Williams' number from the church flyer and put my number on there. I let Bishop know that in reality, Ashley suggested that I put my contact information on the flyer since I was the outreach leader. I told her that we should leave it like it was. They then called Ashley into the office. She stood there and lied on me in my face. I just glared at her across the room. She couldn't even look up and meet my gaze because she knew it was a lie. So, after being threatened and lied on, I was released to leave. I drove home in tears as I wondered what I could do to get back in Bishop's good graces. When I got home I sent him a text.

"Praise the Lord Bishop." it read. "I just want to repent to you for making you upset tonight..."

That incident kicked off the drama starting up again. Ashley and I got texts one night saying to meet up at Bishop's apartment. When we got there, we found out it was a rebuking session. The victim was Brian. He did something to upset Bishop, so we had to sit through Bishop going off on him for hours. Ashley, Pastor Williams, and I had to chime in and say what Brian had done to offend us. Bishop rehashed everything that Brian had ever done wrong. He even brought up things that had happened in Atlanta. The session finally finished around six in the morning.

Thankfully, it wasn't a rebuking session every time we were summoned to Bishop's place. He would get in these good moods sometimes and want us to come have fun instead of getting rebuked. It would be fun but still stressful. We usually watched a movie first. Bishop loved horror movies. He would make us watch things with violence and nudity but monitored what we watched and listened to on our own. I threw out all my music that wasn't gospel because he told me to. It was mostly old school music that wasn't vulgar, but I threw it away to please him. Pastor Williams told me early on how when he submitted to Bishop he changed whatever Bishop said to change. He told me we had to obey our "Man of God" in all things, so we could make it to heaven. Anyway, Ashley and I felt convicted about watching horror movies. We would look away or cover our eyes at bad parts. Bishop would actually make fun of us and say we were being "too deep". He would have gone off on us if we watched something he was uncomfortable with in his presence. He rebuked us one night at a sister's house because we were watching the BET Awards.

After watching a movie, we would play UNO. Anytime we played UNO, we had to let Bishop win. He would get so angry if someone made him draw cards or altogether beat him. We also played our own version of the dozens while playing cards. We would dog each other out by joking on each other. It was all in good fun though. Even though we were joking on each other, we knew from previous experience not to joke on Bishop. He could dish it, but couldn't take it. It was because of his insecurities. To those on the outside, he seemed so confident and put together. Those closest to him knew that in private, he was far from having it together.

Things were continued to unravel with Brian and me. He was still living with me, and I was shouldering the burden of the mortgage and bills on my own. He kept losing jobs. He lost one job because he called out to travel with Bishop.

One night Bishop called Brian and told him he was sick and at the emergency room. He was testing Brian's loyalty as usual. And as usual, Brian fell for it. He immediately headed out on foot in the snow without telling me what was going on. A few minutes later, Bishop called and told me what he said to Brian. He hollered laughing when I told him that Brian was walking in the snow to get to him. He then informed me that Brian had received his income tax and told him he wasn't giving me a dime. He and Pastor Williams went on and on about how low down he was for not giving me any money. I got mad and called Brian to ask him about it.

"Hey I heard you got your income tax today," I said when he answered.

"And?" he asked with an attitude.

"I need you to help me pay some of these bills! You live here too. I shouldn't have to do it all by myself!" I yelled.

"Child please," he said before hanging up on me.

I immediately called Bishop back to tell him what Brian did. I was so angry. I went in the living room and flung open the closet door. I stood there and looked at all his belongings.

"I ought to just throw all his stuff outside in the snow," I threatened.

"I'd do it if I were you. You better than me. I couldn't have a lazy negro laying up in my house eating all my food and using my heat."

Bishop kept egging me on to throw the stuff out until I eventually started grabbing his things and throwing them out. I threw out all of his clothes, shoes, books, etc. Once everything was in the yard, I took a picture of it and sent it to Brian. He didn't respond.

The next morning when I woke up, I saw that Brian didn't come home the night before. I felt horrible about throwing his belongings out. My dad and my close friend advised me to get his stuff out of the yard, bag it up, and ask him to come get it. He came and picked up his items the next day. He didn't speak to me. He just grabbed his bags and left to go stay with Ashley. Imagine my surprise when days later, Bishop calls to rebuke me for throwing Brian's clothes outside. He said Brian was distraught because his white suit had mud on it. I ended up having Brian's suit dry-cleaned after that. We eventually had a meeting in which we apologized to each other. I felt bad for what I did, but I couldn't believe Bishop was mad at me. He was the one that encouraged me to do it.

Things began to really unravel for Brian. He was involved in a scandal on social media when the person that he was dating posted a picture of him naked. The picture was from the neck down, but I could tell that it was Brian. Of course, he denied that it was him. Bishop was livid when he found out about it. He was embarrassed that a minister from our church was naked on the internet. Most of the people we fellowshipped with in other cities and states saw the picture. He was also upset about who Brian was dating. He knew the person and didn't like them. He really didn't want any of us, especially Brian, dating anyone still. It cut into our devotion to him. The ministers went to dinner with Bishop that night to discuss the scandal. Brian repented to everyone, and we thought it was over. However, when we got in the parking lot Pastor Williams exploded on Bishop.

"I can't believe this! He's getting away with something again. You never hold him responsible when he does something stupid!" he yelled at Bishop.

"Who you yelling at negro?! I am still your pastor. And for your information, I do hold him responsible. Why do you think we had this meeting?"

They went back and forth arguing. I noticed that Brian was always a sore spot between them. He just stood there silently with me as we watched our pastors argue. Finally, I was released to go. I went home and went to bed. I was physically and mentally exhausted from that day's events.

Around one o'clock in the morning, my phone started ringing. It was Bishop.

"Hello." I answered groggily.

"You need to come over here and get this n***a! He done lost his mind!" Bishop yelled.

"Where are you? What's going on?" I asked sitting up in the bed.

"We're at the Circle C at Mastin Lake and Blue Springs. Me and Pastor Williams just got in a fight."

"A fight?!"

"Yes a fight. I hemmed him up for talking to me crazy. You need to get over here right now!" he ordered before hanging up.

I climbed out of bed, got dressed, and headed over to the Circle C. When I pulled up, I saw Bishop and Pastor Williams standing next to Bishop's car yelling and making wild gestures. Brian was standing off to the side looking at the ground. I parked and got out of my car.

"What's going on? Are y'all okay?" I asked as I walked up.

"Your assistant pastor over here coming at me crazy. I'm sick of this mess!" Bishop yelled.

"That's fine! I'm taking my stuff and leaving! I am tired of being disrespected by you. I don't have to take this." Pastor Williams confessed as he opened the trunk of their car. He began throwing things in a black duffle bag that he had pulled out of the car.

"I don't care. Leave!" Bishop yelled as Pastor Williams threw items in his bag.

Pastor Williams then shut the trunk, slung the bag on his shoulder, and started off down the road walking. Brian and I just stood there stunned.

"Oh so you're really going to leave?!" Bishop yelled as he started walking down the street after Pastor Williams.

I don't know what was said because they were down the road, but Pastor Williams stopped and talked to Bishop. After a few minutes, they returned to where Brian and I stood.

"It's all good. Go on home, and get some rest honey." Bishop said as he and Pastor Williams got in the car. Brian got in with them, and they drove off. The next morning we were all in church shouting like nothing had happened.

Shortly after that, Bishop's parents suffered a house fire. Bishop and Pastor Williams had just moved to Muscle Shoals to live with them after losing their apartment. Now, they all were living in a hotel. Brian and I went down there every evening when I got off from work to make sure they had dinner and to run errands. A couple of times, we drove down there in snow and ice to make sure we were there for Bishop and Pastor Williams. Sometimes Ashley would go with us. Brian and Ashley were Bishop's personal armor bearer and handmaiden respectively. By this time, I served sometimes as Mother Davis' armor bearer. I would have to follow her around and accompany her to the bathroom when we were out. I had to stand on guard outside the door and hold her purse.

During this time, we were having church at the hotel where Bishop was living. This meant we all had to drive from Huntsville to Muscle Shoals every Sunday for church. Eventually, Bishop's parents, along with Bishop and Pastor Williams, moved into an apartment while their house was being repaired. We had church in that apartment for awhile. Some of those services were a little wild.

One night we were having a ladies' bible study at the apartment which was led by Mother Davis. She was right in the middle of teaching when we heard glass breaking, bumping against the wall, and yelling. Mother Davis jumped up to go and see what was happening. A moment later, she quickly came back into the living room where we were.

"Y'all pray! Pray right now!" she said frantically.

We all immediately began to pray. We had no idea what had happened. We didn't know if anyone was hurt. After we prayed, Bishop and Pastor Williams came walking out of the back.

"Praise the Lord y'all!" Bishop spat with an attitude.

"Praise the Lord," we all mumbled in response.

Pastor Williams barely spoke as he walked out of the door. Bishop went and sat down in a chair in the corner and started doing something on his phone. I got up and went over to make sure he was okay.

"You alright?" I asked as I approached him.

"Yeah honey. I'm alright," he answered. "Go look at my bedroom though."

I walked back to his bedroom and was stunned to see broken glass all over the floor. Items had been knocked from the dresser. There clearly had been another fight between Bishop and Pastor Williams. I couldn't believe my pastors had interrupted our bible study with a fistfight.

Church wasn't the only reason for frequent visits to the Muscle Shoals area. We were back and forth a lot because Bishop was in and out of the hospital. He constantly went through so much in his body because of diabetes. Anytime he was hospitalized or even went to the emergency room, we all were required to stop what we were doing and be there. If we didn't come visit him every day in the hospital, there would be a price to pay. Once when he was in the hospital, he texted me and asked me to come to see him. He also told me to bring Ashley and Brian. I explained that I was having car trouble and couldn't get down there that night. I told him I would try to find a way to Florence in the next couple of days. In response, he sent me back a picture of himself lying in the hospital bed. He had a sad look on his face and tubes attached to him. The text with the picture was him going in on me about not caring whether he lived or died. He called me "selfish as usual" for not getting on the road immediately and coming to see about him. Of course, I felt horrible. I made sure to secure a ride for the next two days to go visit him.

During the spring and summer, we continued to travel with Bishop doing revivals. Bishop also continued to be in and out of the hospital. While in the hospital, he made another appearance on *Crime Stoppers* with Brian for writing bad checks. Shortly after this incident, I was hanging with Brian one night. We were watching the Juanita Bynum sermon "No More Sheets." Brian turned and looked at me with so much sadness in his eyes.

"Tracie, I'm so tired of the sheets in my life," he expressed sadly.

"Brian, you're gonna be alright. Whatever has you bound, you can come out of it. God has so many good things planned for you." I assured him.

"I guess so," he agreed.

The next day, I was on my way home from work when I spotted Brian walking on the sidewalk. I pulled up and picked him up. He had a bandage wrapped around his arm. He explained that he had just come from giving plasma for money. We road along and had small talk. I could tell something was bothering him. I dropped him off at my house, so he could rest. I told him that I was going to run an errand and would be right back. When I got back to my house about twenty minutes later, Brian was gone. I looked in the front closet, and none of his things were in there. I immediately called Bishop.

"Brian left. All of his stuff is gone." I told him.

It then dawned on me why Brian had given plasma to get money. He had already planned on running away. Of course, Bishop was very hurt and upset. He was especially upset because, we were leaving in the morning to go to Arkansas for a revival service. He couldn't stop talking about it and being angry. I had never seen him take somebody leaving so hard. Secretly, I was glad for Brian getting away from Bishop and the church.

The next person to go was another minister, Min. Gary, whom I still consider my brother today. It all began to unravel when we got back from Arkansas around 4 o'clock in the morning. We pulled up to the hotel where Bishop told me to leave my car and found that my car was gone. I ran inside to ask the lady at the front desk if she knew anything about my car. She said that it had been towed the day before. She gave me the name and number of the towing company. I walked back outside to tell everyone what happened.

"My car was towed! I don't know how Ashley and I are going to get home." I said frantically.

"That's a mess honey." Bishop admitted. "Well, y'all call me in the morning and let me know you're ok."

He then rolled his window up and Pastor Williams drove off. I stood there with tears in my eyes as they drove away. I couldn't believe that he didn't care that we were stranded in Muscle Shoals without a car and nowhere to stay. I would never have done that to him. Thankfully, Min. Gary had his car. He checked us all into a motel. He even offered to sleep in the lobby to make sure Ashley and I were comfortable. Of course, we insisted he stay in the room with us. The next day, he paid to get my car back from the towing company. I will be forever grateful for his kindness to us. After that incident, Bishop began trying to run Min. Gary away. I couldn't believe it because Min. Gary had been with the church from the beginning. He finally succeeded one night during a meeting at Bishop's house. Min. Gary had called in since he lived in Birmingham. After Bishop said things to humiliate him, the minister decided that enough was enough.

"I'm quitting the ministry. I can't do this anymore. I love you all and God bless you," he said as he abruptly hung up the phone.

For the rest of the summer, more members continued to leave. Finally, it dwindled down to seven of us. Bishop then began to assign us to people whom he wanted recruited into the ministry. He began to work on members from a church that we regularly fellowshipped with. Their pastor was similar to Bishop. Everyone at their church dressed alike and worshipped their pastor. We actually got that pastor's niece to leave and come to our church after the pastor tried to force her into an arranged marriage. I felt bad for the young girl because she didn't realize that she would be facing drama and foolishness at our church as well.

Bishop also began to pressure me to bring one of my new friends from work into the ministry. I would pray that she wouldn't even visit. Her friendship was such a refuge for me, and I didn't want the church to mess that up. Thankfully, she never came.

By the end of July, Bishop was in the hospital again. One night, he asked those that were left to come to visit him and have a prayer meeting at the hospital chapel. After prayer,

Bishop addressed us all one by one. He told us how much he loved us and that he was excited for all that God had planned for us. It was very emotional. While he was speaking, I had an eerie feeling that I couldn't explain or shake.

In August, we were beginning to see membership pick back up since we had begun having services at a hotel in Decatur. One of my friends from work and his family had even joined our church one Sunday evening. During that same service, Bishop preached about repentance and going to heaven. He had been preaching on heaven a few services in a row. That night after church, I approached his car to say goodbye.

"I'm tired," he said wearily.

"Well, go get in the bed and get some rest." I suggested.

"No Tracie. I'm tired," he repeated.

He had a weird look in his eyes. He looked tired but sad. I just shook it off and told him good night. Later that night, he called me to talk as usual. We talked about so much for hours. He even talked me about a lady whom he was interested in. We had all met her when Bishop invited her and her mother to church. I told him that I thought she was a great person. I was glad that he and I had come to a point where we could talk about being with other people and there not be any jealousy. I hung up with him that night and had no idea that I would never talk to him again.

The following Wednesday, Bishop went back into the hospital. Bible study was cancelled and we were told to just pray. Around 2:00 in the morning, I received a text from Pastor Williams saying that there had been an emergency and to bombard heaven with prayer for Bishop. I immediately got up and began to intercede. After I prayed, I still felt heaviness. I later found out that the emergency was that Bishop had gone into emergency surgery to have an infection removed from his foot. He had died on the operating table but, was resuscitated. He then lapsed into a diabetic coma and was placed on life support.

That Friday, Pastor Williams and Mother Davis called and told me and Ashley to get to the hospital quickly. Bishop was getting worse. There were already rumors that he was brain dead. We immediately got on the road and headed to the hospital in Florence. We spent the night at the hospital to make sure we were there to assist Bishop's parents and Pastor Williams. In the middle of the night, there was a flurry of activity when a nurse burst into the sleeping area and told Bishop's parents and Pastor Williams to come with them. Ashley and I got up and began to pray. A few hours later, we all got together at the chapel to pray together. I still couldn't shake the heaviness that I felt. Later that morning, I headed back to Huntsville, so that I could go to work. I assured Pastor Williams that I would be back after work.

After work, I was exhausted. Talking to crazy customers and a lack of sleep had me ready to crash into the nearest bed. I called Pastor Williams and let him know that Ashley and I would come in the morning. Surprisingly, he didn't get mad. He told me to rest and he would see me in the morning.

That next morning, Ashley and I made our way to Florence. On the way there, a minister whom we fellowshipped with called me.

"Praise the Lord Evangelist. I'm so sorry to hear that Bishop Davis passed. Are you ok?" she asked.

I was stunned, but that soon turned to anger.

"Bishop isn't dead." I told her with an attitude. "Ashley and I are on our way to the hospital to see him now.

"Oh. I'm sorry. I must have misunderstood. Tell everyone I'm praying for them," she said.

After we hung up, I told Ashley what the minister had said. We both were upset because, people had been spreading rumors about the situation. About fifteen minutes before we reached Muscle Shoals, Pastor Williams called and said to meet him at the apartment instead of the hospital. When we reached the apartment, Pastor Williams told us to get in his car. As soon as we got into the back of the car, Pastor Williams turned around in his seat to face us.

"Bishop passed away this morning," he confirmed.

Ashley and I immediately began to scream and cry. I felt like my heart was literally breaking. Bishop had his flaws, but he was one of the closest people to me. I felt sick and dizzy as Ashley and I held each other and cried. I then noticed what I hadn't when I first got in. Pastor Williams' eyes were red and swollen from crying. I felt so bad for him because he was the closest to Bishop out of all of us. Even though Pastor Williams was hurting, he was concerned about us.

Once we calmed down, Pastor Williams explained that Bishop's parents had decided to take him off of life support. He said that they were still at the hospital. We spent the rest of the afternoon riding around Decatur with Pastor Williams to inform several people that Bishop had passed and to ask for money to help with funeral and burial expenses. Ashley and I were given a list of people to call in surrounding cities and states. I numbly called number after number. I was in disbelief that when we should have been processing Bishop's death, we were on the phone begging for money. It was business as usual. Most of the people we called were pastors and former members that Bishop had fallen out with over one thing or another. It was usually Bishop's fault. At that point, we hadn't spoken to most of these people in awhile. Although it was awkward, everyone was caring and compassionate.

When we finally got back to Bishop's parents' apartment, many of his family members had already gathered there. Ashley and I were expected to serve and entertain which I wasn't in the mood to do. Although I smiled on the outside, on the inside my heart was broken, and I felt lost on the inside. What was I going to do without Bishop? Who was I without him? Who would lead us now? We had such a sick and twisted dependency on him.

The morning after he died was so hard. I woke up checking my phone to make sure I hadn't missed any calls or texts from Bishop. Then, it hit me all over again that he was gone. That week was spent crying, consoling Pastor Williams, and going back and forth to Muscle Shoals to be with Bishop's parents.

That Wednesday night, we all gathered at Bishop's parents' apartment to discuss the funeral arrangements. I noticed that while the plans were discussed, Pastor Williams wasn't included in anything. As a matter of fact, Pastor Williams spent most of the meeting outside on the phone. I was the only minister that was asked to participate by reading a scripture at the beginning of the service. I noticed the day of Bishop's death that there was tension between his parents and Pastor Williams. I was sitting outside with Bishop's father and we were talking about Bishop's death.

"I wish my son didn't have to die, but I am so glad to finally get this sorry n***a, Alan, out of my house," he confessed. "I only let him stay here to keep peace with my son."

I didn't know what to say in response to that. I was stunned because Bishop's parents had always referred to Pastor Williams as their other son. I had no idea that they really didn't care for him. I could certainly understand Bishop's father's feelings. Pastor Williams and I had experienced conflict between us since I joined the ministry.

That Friday evening, we, the family and remaining members, made our way to the funeral home for the family hour. I felt sick on the drive over thinking about seeing Bishop in his casket. I had not seen him since the week before his death. When we entered the funeral home, Ashley and I grabbed hands and walked together into the viewing room. We took a deep breath and walked up to the casket. As soon as I saw him, the room began to spin. Ashley fainted. I felt like I couldn't breathe so I turned and ran outside. When I got outside, I began to scream and cry. I was begging God to help me wake up from the nightmare that was my reality. I wasn't sure if I could go on without Bishop.

The next morning was the funeral. As Ashley and I stood at the door greeting guests, former members and pastors we used to fellowship with began to show up. We may have had our differences in the past because of Bishop but in that moment we were family again. Ashley and I cried as each person embraced us and offered words of encouragement. It was such a blessing to see everyone although I wished it was for a different reason. They will never know how much their support meant that day.

Bishop had a very joyous home going. Many ministers got up and said very touching words about him. Even people whom he had fallen out with in the past. I kept fighting feelings of guilt. Although I was very sad about his passing, I began to feel a relief that he was gone. I couldn't understand or process my feelings at that point, so I pushed them down deeply. I didn't want to be disloyal to him even in death.

The hardest part of the day was the burial. I felt numb as I watched the workers begin to shovel dirt onto the casket. Soon, everyone began to leave because it was so hard to watch. However, Ashley and I stood there with Pastor Williams until the last piece of dirt was shoveled. When they were done, it felt so final. I had stood with Bishop until the very end. It was in that moment that I felt a release from the ministry. I chose to ignore my feelings and fight to maintain loyalty to Bishop even though I knew my time was up there. The feeling got stronger though as we said our goodbyes to the former members later on that evening. I felt jealous as I watched everyone drive away in freedom. Ashley and I had to stay and be released by Pastor Williams to go home. It was now understood that Pastor Williams had stepped into Bishop's shoes according to the church by-laws. Now, we were his armor bearers.

The next afternoon, the ministers met at Bishop's parents' house to discuss moving on with the church following Bishop's death. We agreed to continue with having church at the hotel in Decatur. Immediately after the meeting, confusion evolved. Ashley, Pastor Williams, Mother Davis, and I went to have dinner after the meeting. After dinner, I pulled Pastor Williams to the side to talk to him. I gave him some money since he didn't have anything. He didn't have a car or a job. Soon, he wouldn't have a place to live. I also let him know that he had my full support as the new pastor.

Later that evening, Mother Davis called me. We ended up having a bizarre conversation.

"Praise the Lord Evangelist Winn. This is Pastor Davis," she greeted me. "I wanted to ask you what you and Pastor Williams discussed outside after dinner. I need to know everything that's going on since I'm the pastor now."

I was stunned. I then respectfully reminded her that Bishop had said in the by-laws that Pastor Williams would be pastor if he died. She then let me know that Bishop changed the by-laws while hospitalized. That confused me because he was in a coma while in the hospital. I decided to just go along with what she was saying. I felt that maybe she was so devastated by losing Bishop that she wasn't thinking clearly. I hung up with her and told Ashley what was said. She agreed that it was probably the grief talking.

The following Wednesday, Pastor Williams called a church meeting in Muscle Shoals. On the way to the meeting, Mother Davis called.

"Are you still coming to the meeting tonight?" she asked.

"Yes ma'am. Sis and I are almost at the restaurant." I answered.

"Honey, the meeting is at my house," she said.

"Oh. Pastor Williams said we were going to Shoney's." I said. "Did something change?"

"The meeting is going to be at the apartment. I will see y'all in a bit."

"Ok then. Bye."

I hung up feeling confused all over again. I called Pastor Williams and he let me know he was at the restaurant waiting on us. We knew something wasn't right. When we got to the restaurant, Pastor Williams was there along with a pastor that was a close friend of Bishop's. Pastor Williams explained that he went over the by-laws with Mother Davis and she still insisted that she was the pastor. She convinced the other members to take her side and they chose to go to her meeting. As Ashley and I left Muscle Shoals, I told her that I was seriously thinking about leaving the church. I was just so tired of the constant drama. I didn't even have the strength to answer when Mother Davis called later that evening. I knew she would want to know why I sided with Pastor Williams over her. I really wasn't choosing sides. I just wanted to do what was right and honor Bishop's wishes.

The next evening while I was in class, Mother Davis left a weird voicemail on my phone.

"Praise the Lord Evangelist. This is Pastor Davis. I need to know if you plan to continue with us as an evangelist and prayer warrior. If you don't plan to stay, then I need to replace you. Tracie, we do love you and hope to hear from you soon."

When I heard that voicemail, I knew that I was finished. I called her the next evening and let her know that I was officially resigning from the church. I told her that I loved her and Bishop's father, but I had to move on. I never spoke to either one of them again. Mother Davis passed away a couple of years later.

A couple of weeks after leaving, Ashley and I joined a church in Huntsville. By this point, Pastor Williams wasn't speaking to either one of us. We parted ways with him because he was still trying to bring drama and mess to our lives. Finally, Ashley and I decided to discuss all that we had been through in the ministry. It was as if someone had opened a floodgate. We talked for hours about our true feelings, our hurt, disappointment, and shame from getting caught up for so long in a church like that. There is no way I could have made it through that time without Ashley. We were a big support to each other. Once we admitted that we had been abused, we wanted to talk about it a lot and sort through our feelings. I thank God for my friends and family that listened and tried to be there. It was just hard for them because they didn't understand.

It has taken literally years to heal from all of the hurt, confusion, guilt, and shame. I had to pray, trust God, and take it one day at a time. Some days I would just break down and cry. I would cry when I thought of all I lost, including four years, because of it. I had to deal with triggers daily. So many things would trigger memories in my mind and put me right back in the place I fought so hard to escape from. It could be the way someone spoke to me or even the smell of certain colognes that would trigger bad memories for me. I also had to go back and sort through the false doctrine that I had been taught. I had to search the Bible and find out what I believed all over again. I had to regain my confidence and relearn how to make my own decisions. I had to find my own individual style outside of how Bishop wanted me to dress. It still took years to find me, but that's another book! However, I am a witness that God can and will heal all wounds if we give the situation over to him. You cannot heal from something like this alone. It helped me tremendously to talk to a Christian counselor. She helped me to sort through all of my feelings and get to a place of healing. It started with writing a letter to Bishop. I said everything in that letter that I wasn't able to say while he was alive. I expressed my anger, hurt, and bitterness. I pray that God would bring healing, peace, and courage to every individual that is suffering or has suffered from spiritual abuse. I pray also for the families that are hurting from a loved being involved with an abusive group. May God bless you on your journey!

Ten Signs of Cult/Spiritual Abuse

1. Love Bombing

"Love Bombing" refers to the overwhelming response of love and friendliness a visitor is shown during initial interactions with the church. In our church it was called the "Anointed Revival Center Welcome". Pastor would instruct us to greet our guests. Therefore, we would then descend the visitors with hugs, upbeat greetings, and smiles. We would also exchange phone numbers with them. Since I was the outreach leader, I was mostly responsible for befriending guests. I would usually reach out to them the next day and convince them to come back to the church again. Meanwhile, we would also invite guests out to eat and to any other church outings so that they could get acquainted with us. We wanted each person to see that we were a big happy family that would accept him or her. Once someone joined the excessive attention would taper off, and we would move on to the next person.

2. Isolation/Division

After joining an abusive church, the pastor usually works on isolating a person from family and friends. For instance Pastor would put me in situations where I had to choose between him and my family. Then, he would make it seem like I was disloyal to him and to God. He would also repeatedly tell me that my parents didn't love me or support my ministry like he did. Meanwhile, he would preach unity, but behind closed doors it was another story. Unfortunately, he worked hard to break down my friendships with those inside and outside of the church by sowing discord and causing confusion. My former pastor would keep so much drama and gossip going between members that we really didn't like or trust each other most of the time. He also didn't want me around anyone who could see him for whom he really was and risk them talking me out of following him. He eventually made it to where I was very dependent on him alone, even more than God.

3. Manipulation

Abusive pastors will draw people through manipulation disguised as flattery. They will tell you how wonderful and anointed you are. To seal the deal, they will quickly tell you that you are called to ministry and give you a title. They want you to feel very important. Next, you enter ministry training where you will be asked to be an armor bearer (i.e. a slave to the pastor). This makes the person feel special because, he or she has access to the pastor that others in the church don't have.

Soon after, you will be assimilated into the ministry through your clothing and speech. You will quickly learn "church talk". These are words and phrases associated with the church. Most emphasis will be placed on your outward appearance. You will be taught what is and isn't acceptable to wear. Doing the wrong thing can bring harsh rebuke from the pastor. You quickly fall in line in order to avoid being the odd person that isn't doing what everyone else is.

4. Leader Worship

In churches where spiritual abuse occurs, the pastor is the main focal point. He is set up as an idol to the people as they look to him for guidance on everything from what job to take to what to wear. Everything in the church revolves around the pastor. Nothing can be done without his approval. He will set up leaders but end up taking over the tasks he has delegated to others. The members are conditioned over time to worship the pastor through giving of money, gifts, time, and adoration. Giving in itself is not wrong, but it can be when one gives in order to be accepted by the pastor. If you find yourself talking about your pastor more than God, you might be in an abusive situation.

5. Don't Ask/Don't Talk

"Don't ask/don't talk" is a tactic that is used by controlling pastors to ensure loyalty from the members at all times. At my former church, people who asked questions or voiced their concerns were seen as rebels causing trouble. From time to time, someone like this would join the ministry and leave a few months later in frustration. When I first joined, I was one of those people. Finally, I realized that not talking to anybody about my concerns was the best way to keep peace and not cause trouble, even if I had to suffer in silence. I also proved my loyalty by keeping quiet when questioned about things that were going on in our church by outsiders. Therefore, I would vaguely answer questions, if I answered them at all. We were taught to cover our leader no matter what. That's why I constantly defended his wrong. Even after my pastor died, it took awhile for me to speak about what happened at our church because I felt like I was betraying him.

6. Us vs. Them

Many abusive churches have a major "us versus them" mentality. My pastor was suspicious of anyone outside of our church-even some of his close friends who regularly fellowshipped with us. He would put down and gossip about other pastors and churches out of jealousy. As a result, he destroyed many friendships this way. He also looked at everything as persecution. When there was concern from our family members and other churches, it was called persecution. When members of our church appeared on the news after being arrested for committing crimes, he told us that the media and cops were against our church. He always told us that the only people whom we could trust to have our backs were other church members. He would tell us that our families and friends didn't understand our church because they weren't saved. He felt like anybody who said he/she was a Christian but didn't believe exactly like him was going to hell.

7. Disfellowship

Disfellowship occurs when someone leaves the ministry or is put out by the pastor. The remaining church members have to behave as if the person has died. In our church, we had to erase former members' numbers and not have any contact with them whatsoever. My pastor was the only one who could remain in contact with those whom left. According to my pastor, anyone who was no longer a member was referred to as a "bastard" since he/she no longer had a father. However, that person could be received again if he/she repented to Pastor and the church during church service.

8. Recruitment

Recruitment into an abusive church is disguised as witnessing. I remember times where I was assigned to bring certain people into the church. For example, Pastor once assigned me to some members of a church whom we normally fellowshipped with. We actually convinced one of them to leave their church to come with us. My pastor was very aggressive when it came to getting someone to join our church. He would use whatever tactics that were necessary. He used the "you're my wife" line with me and many other women of the church. Therefore, be cautious when a pastor or church members pressure you to join a church. That's something that shouldn't be forced.

9. False Doctrine

Controlling pastors will keep members in line with fear through false doctrine. They will twist certain scriptures in order to keep members in line. My former pastor had certain scriptures that he would often use to manipulate us. He had scriptures on submitting to authority, giving money to him, and justification for public embarrassment. He would also have us fearful that every mistake would send us to hell. Inasmuch, he would constantly tell us "y'all are gonna bust hell wide open." According to him, we were constantly in danger of losing our salvation. As a result, wore ourselves out trying to be perfect for him. We would get so discouraged and depressed when we let him down because that meant we let God down too.

Some of the scriptures he used to control us are as follow:

Hebrews 13:17 - Obey them that have the rule over you, and submit yourselves: for they watch for your souls, as they that must give account, that they may do it with joy, and not with grief: for that is unprofitable for you.

Proverbs 27:5 - Open rebuke is better than secret love.

1 Timothy 5:20 - Them that sin rebuke before all, that others also may fear.

1 Timothy 5:18 - For the scripture saith, Thou shalt not muzzle the ox that treadeth out the corn. And, the labourer is worthy of his reward.

Matthew 10:41 - He that receiveth a prophet in the name of a prophet shall receive a prophet's reward; and he that receiveth a righteous man in the name of a righteous man shall receive a righteous man's reward.

1 Timothy 5:17 - Let the elders that rule well be counted worthy of double honour, especially they who labour in the word and doctrine.

Psalm 105:15 - *Saying*, Touch not mine anointed, and do my prophets no harm.

Malachi 3:8-10 -Will a man rob God? Yet ye have robbed me. But ye say, Wherein have we robbed thee? In tithes and offerings. Ye *are* cursed with a curse: for ye have robbed me, *even* this whole nation. Bring ye all the tithes into the storehouse, that there may be meat in mine house, and prove me now herewith, saith the LORD of hosts, if I will not open you the windows of heaven, and pour you out a blessing, that *there shall* not *be room* enough *to receive it.*

Exodus 17:11 - And it came to pass, when Moses held up his hand, that Israel prevailed: and when he let down his hand, Amalek prevailed.

10.   Moving/Name Change

Abusive churches/cults constantly move. I referred to those of us in my former church as "spiritual gypsies" and our church as a "circus church". This name came from the fact that we sometimes had church in a different place every week. It was usually in a place where we had to set everything up and take it down. We had to constantly move due to getting evicted and being too noisy. Wherever the church moved, we all would follow, even if it was to another city.

We also had to change our name due to bad publicity surrounding our church when our pastor and some members kept getting arrested for crime. Although, my pastor claimed God told him to change the name, I never believed that.

Tracie Winn is a minister, writer, and actor from Huntsville, AL. She is the founder of Beauty for Ashes Outreach Ministry. She is an acting teacher at Maitland Conservatory. She is also the creator and director of Scenes of a Single Sister Web series.

Proof

Made in the USA
Columbia, SC
27 April 2017